Momfulness

JB JOSSEY-BASS

Momfulness

Mothering with Mindfulness, Compassion, and Grace

Denise Roy

BICENTENNIAL
1807
WILEY
2007
BICENTENNIAL

John Wiley & Sons

Published by Jossey-Bass
A Wiley Imprint
989 Market Street, San Francisco, CA 94103-1741 www.josseybass.com

No part of this publication may be reproduced, stored in a retrieval system, or transmitted in any form or by any means, electronic, mechanical, photocopying, recording, scanning, or otherwise, except as permitted under Section 107 or 108 of the 1976 United States Copyright Act, without either the prior written permission of the publisher, or authorization through payment of the appropriate per-copy fee to the Copyright Clearance Center, Inc., 222 Rosewood Drive, Danvers, MA 01923, 978-750-8400, fax 978-646-8600, or on the Web at www.copyright.com. Requests to the publisher for permission should be addressed to the Permissions Department, John Wiley & Sons, Inc., 111 River Street, Hoboken, NJ 07030, 201-748-6011, fax 201-748-6008, or online at http://www.wiley.com/go/permissions.

Limit of Liability/Disclaimer of Warranty: While the publisher and author have used their best efforts in preparing this book, they make no representations or warranties with respect to the accuracy or completeness of the contents of this book and specifically disclaim any implied warranties of merchantability or fitness for a particular purpose. No warranty may be created or extended by sales representatives or written sales materials. The advice and strategies contained herein may not be suitable for your situation. You should consult with a professional where appropriate. Neither the publisher nor author shall be liable for any loss of profit or any other commercial damages, including but not limited to special, incidental, consequential, or other damages.

Readers should be aware that Internet Web sites offered as citations and/or sources for further information may have changed or disappeared between the time this was written and when it is read. Jossey-Bass books and products are available through most bookstores. To contact Jossey-Bass directly call our Customer Care Department within the U.S. at 800-956-7739, outside the U.S. at 317-572-3986, or fax 317-572-4002.

Jossey-Bass also publishes its books in a variety of electronic formats. Some content that appears in print may not be available in electronic books.

Credits are on page 241.

Library of Congress Cataloging-in-Publication Data
Roy, Denise, Date.
Momfulness : mothering with mindfulness, compassion, and grace / Denise Roy.
p. cm.
Includes bibliographical references.
ISBN-13: 978-0-7879-8197-6 (pbk.)
ISBN-10: 0-7879-8197-4 (pbk.)
1. Motherhood. 2. Mothers—Psychology. 3. Mothers—Conduct of life. I. Title
HQ759.R694   2007
204'.41—dc22   2006030497

Printed in the United States of America
FIRST EDITION
PB Printing 10 9 8 7 6 5 4 3 2

Contents

To all who bring the passion of a mother
to their work on behalf of the children
and of the planet

Introduction

So there I was, twenty-seven-years old, waddling down the aisle to the front of the church to receive my diploma. I carried my eighteen-month-old son in my arms and my soon-to-be-born second son in my belly.

After four years of studying at a seminary, I was receiving a Master of Divinity degree. I wanted to be a minister, to put into practice the teachings and values of love, compassion, forgiveness, peace. What I was just beginning to grasp, as a very new mother, was that my spiritual practice was ultimately not going to involve preaching to a choir but, rather, preaching to my kids! It was not going to take place primarily in a church, breaking bread and sharing wine; more often than not, it was going to take place in the kitchen serving up graham crackers and chocolate milk.

As the mother of four children (and the foster mom of a fifth), I can attest to the fact that motherhood leaves stretch marks on us—in so many ways! I have been stretched physically, mentally, emotionally, spiritually. My limited notion of what constitutes a family has widened, and I have been pulled (sometimes kicking and screaming) into the present moment. Through great challenges and even greater love, my heart has grown to hold more than I ever thought possible.

Motherhood continues to stretch me to this day, and I see no end in sight. It teaches lessons that many spiritual disciplines teach: the transforming effect of true presence, the importance of close attention, the need for deep compassion, the celebration of embodiment, the recognition of the sacred in all things, and the power of community.

Momfulness is the word I use for this spiritual practice of conscious mothering. When we mother with mindfulness and compassion and a willingness to let this vocation awaken our hearts and transform our lives, we walk a spiritual path. We discover that care for our children and family is not a distraction from sacred practice but is the very essence of it.

My husband and I conceived of the word *Momfulness* at (appropriately enough) our kitchen table, and since then I keep discovering more and more what it means to be Momful. My oldest son Ben calls it entering the "mama zone." That may be as good a characterization as any. Words can't capture its full meaning, because Momfulness is best understood through experience. The reflections and practices in this book are designed so that you can deepen conscious mothering in your own life.

And so I invite you to join me in exploring the spiritual practice of Momfulness, whether in the midst of sticky kisses or at the point of sheer exhaustion, at the moment when your heart is broken or at the point when it stretches wide open, as together we cultivate a mindful, compassionate, mothering presence with ourselves, with our children, and with our world.

You have to find a mother inside yourself.
We all do. Even if we already have a mother,
we still have to find this part of ourselves inside.

Sue Monk Kidd, *The Secret Life of Bees*

Momfulness

Momfulness

I want to be straight with you. Momfulness is not about perfection. It is also not about motherhood as bliss. Nothing is bliss all the time. I love being a mom, and at the same time, motherhood can be incredibly grueling and frustrating, often pushing me to my limits.

Momfulness is also not about adding another thing to your to-do lists. So if you think you're too busy to engage in a spiritual practice, think again. You can do this right where you are. If you're steeped in dirty diapers, if you're dealing with acting-out teenagers, if you're trying to balance work and home and it feels like you have time for neither, this is the practice for you.

You can't practice Momfulness by sitting on a meditation cushion all day (not that there's much danger of that happening!). Momfulness is practiced in the trenches—while carpooling and cooking, working and waiting, crying and celebrating. Sometimes it will mean carving out moments of solitude and stillness so that you can listen to your heart and your deepest longings, but most of the time it will mean learning how to meditate in motion in the midst of your family life.

A Beginning Definition

So what is Momfulness? Let me offer a beginning definition, and then we'll briefly look at some of the key concepts:

Momfulness is the spiritual practice of cultivating
a mindful, compassionate, mothering presence.

Momfulness Is Mindful

Simply put, mindfulness is being aware of whatever is happening in the present moment without making any judgment. We observe what is happening here, now, including in our own body and mind. Are we feeling boredom? Anger? Fear? Delight? Are we telling ourselves how things should or should not be? Just notice it all. When we are mindful, we become aware and accepting of whatever is there.

What's not so simple is the actual practice of mindfulness. I don't know about you, but I probably spend 98.9 percent of my life not having a clue about what is really happening in this present moment. As moms, we have gazillions of thoughts: we worry, we feel stress, we become attached to life going a certain way. We race from one job to another without being in touch with our bodies or with what we need. Many days we barely make eye contact with our family. We tend to live mindlessly, caught up in the world of our thoughts, judgments, and obligations. We think that this is reality, and we end up missing so much.

See if you can spend a day, or even a few minutes, eavesdropping on your mind. My guess is that you'll discover a continual tape recording going on in your head. You might be thinking about something that happened yesterday, or you might be worrying about something that could happen tomorrow. You might be telling yourself that you're not good enough, smart enough, or thin enough, or that your child is spoiled. Just relax and be curious about it all.

In this book we'll be doing a number of practices that can help us be more mindful in our daily lives. These, however, are just a beginning. There are many other valuable resources that can help you develop a mindfulness practice, and I encourage you to explore some for yourself.

Momfulness Is Compassionate

The English word *compassion* comes from the Latin, meaning "to suffer with." It is defined as a deep awareness of the suffering of another, together with the wish to relieve it. In Hebrew, the word for compassion is *raham,* which comes from the word *rehem,* meaning "womb." To be compassionate is to feel for another with your womb, to hold the person with love, as you might hold a child in your womb.

In practicing Momfulness, we cultivate compassion, not only for others but also for ourselves. We increase our ability to see our own suffering—how tired we are, how hard we are working, how much we don't know. We develop the capacity to forgive ourselves, to love ourselves, and to give ourselves some of what we need. Our hearts open, and we make friends with even the most difficult experiences of our lives.

As we become more tolerant and compassionate with ourselves, we are able to extend that compassion toward our children. We recognize how they suffer, and we are able to better understand what underlies some of their difficult behavior. This awareness increases the chance that we will respond in a helpful, rather than reactive, way.

Our compassion extends beyond our family; we feel in our wombs the suffering of so many in our community and in our world. Rather than let this overwhelm us, we continue to practice, strengthening our capacity to hold suffering instead of avoiding it or numbing ourselves to it. As our hearts open, we awaken into helpful and compassionate action.

Momfulness Is Mothering

Becoming a mother changes us forever. Our psychological, spiritual, physical, and emotional boundaries all undergo a profound shift. As Elizabeth Stone, now a professor at Fordham University, once said, "Making the decision to have a child is momentous. It is to decide forever to have your heart go walking around outside your body." It is no longer only about us. The "I" has become a "we," and nothing is ever the same.

Mothering (in case you don't know!) is not just about apple pie and sweetness. The archetype of Mother is a complex one. Our mothering can be nurturing, protective, and creative—or fierce or destructive, if necessary. In practicing Momfulness, we pay attention to how our mothering might need to shift with various circumstances. We learn how to step into an empowering mothering stance and develop a wide range to our mothering. As poet Zelma Brown articulates:

> I have hands big enough
> to save the world,
> and small enough
> to rock a child to sleep.

In practicing Momfulness, we mother not only our children but also ourselves. When I work with clients (who are mostly moms) in therapy, often the work is in helping them find a mothering and nurturing parent within themselves. Too often their inner voice is a harsh and critical one. As they develop a positive mothering presence within themselves, they are better able to soothe themselves when they are feeling stressed or anxious. Then they are able to mother their own kids in a much more compassionate way.

Momfulness Is About Presence

When I ask moms in seminars, "What is it you long for?" the number one answer I hear is, "More time!" So I pretend to wave a magic wand that gives us all twelve more hours in each day. After the glee and downright giddiness of imagining twelve more hours to nap or exercise or empty the "In" basket or the laundry basket, reality begins to hit the women. They realize that by tomorrow, their calendars would start filling up again, and in about a week or so they'd be complaining that they still don't have enough time. Amazing how quickly those extra hours would disappear!

So, if it's not more time that is the magical solution, what is it? I suggest that much of the problem at the root of our longing lies in the fact that we don't feel really present in the time that we do have. In the limited twenty-four hours of this day, are we showing up? Are we really here? Now? Are we home, in the deepest meaning of that word?

Our ability to be present has a profound effect, not only on the quality of our own lives but on our families' lives as well. As mothers, our interactions with our children quite literally shape the structure and the functions of their brains. This fact alone suggests that the practice of Momfulness, in which we work on connecting with ourselves and with our children in a fully present way, has important long-term implications.

Momfulness Involves Cultivating

Cultivate is a gardening term; it is from the Latin word meaning "to till." Dictionary definitions include "to improve and prepare," "to loosen or dig soil around," "to grow or tend," "to promote the growth of," "to nurture or foster," "to seek the acquaintance of," or "make friends with." All these definitions are apropos to Momfulness: we cultivate a mindful, compassionate, mothering presence. We loosen up the ground within us, we turn it over, we tend it, we promote growth, and we get to know ourselves in a friendly way.

Cultivating, like gardening, is not a linear process, where we start at Point A and move in a straight line to Outcome B (sorry!). Cultivating works with all the earthy elements of life: rainy seasons, droughts, pests, sunshine, weeds, the good, the bad, and the ugly. No matter what happens, it's grist for the mill; we can use it all to our benefit. We simply begin noticing, listening, and observing what's happening inside us and around us, and develop a mind-set that says, "Oh, isn't that interesting!" instead of making judgments about it all.

As we cultivate mindfulness and compassion, we strengthen our ability to understand what we need, what our child needs, what a moment needs. We also begin to realize that we can't pull on growing things to make them come up any sooner. Patience is a key to cultivating things in a healthy way. As you probably already know, patience is one of those qualities of parenting that we will be invited to experience, like it or not, each and every day!

So here we are—cultivating our own little plot of mindfulness, of compassion, of a mothering presence, guided and supported by grace. We practice Momfulness for our children, being mother to them in such a way that they might thrive. We practice Momfulness for ourselves, being a mother to ourselves in such a way that we might thrive. And we practice Momfulness for our world, mobilizing the powerful, fierce, wise, and nurturing mothering presence in such a way that all children—all beings— might thrive.

Why Momfulness Matters

My three sons—all now young adults—were science majors in college. Ben studied neuroscience, Dave received his degree in microbiology, and Matt is completing his studies in biopsychology. I was an English major, and science was never my area of expertise. But I have learned so much from my sons, and now I often find myself interested in scientific findings that shed light on everyday experience. I'd like to share a couple of these with you because I think they underscore the importance of a practice like Momfulness in this day and age.

Stress Is Contagious

Entrainment is the term coined by a Dutch physicist in 1666 who was working on pendulum clocks. He noticed that the pendulums of two clocks, which had been swinging at different rates, began swinging at the same rate if placed in close proximity to each other.

This principle of entrainment, whereby one object affects another so that they begin to move "in sync," is also found in other areas of life. If two heart cells are placed near each other, they will entrain to a common beat. When women live together in close quarters, they discover that their menstrual cycles tend to coincide. When we sit by the ocean, we feel ourselves literally slowing down because we are entraining to the in-and-out, in-and-out, rhythmic movement of the waves.

Now think about times when you lovingly hold your child or partner. Are you aware that your breathing becomes synchronized? You may not know it, but even your heart rates and brain waves are entraining to each other's. Through your close physical connection, you are having a profound effect on one another, literally shaping who the other is becoming.

So far, so good. But if we ask ourselves, *What rhythms are we being entrained to by our modern-day world?* we begin to understand why we are exhausted so much of the time. Technology has transformed our day-to-day lives, filling them with constant noise and speed and way too much information. We live under the influence of powerful, though invisible, rhythms that can, if we're not conscious about them, easily dictate how we live our lives. The stress around us can be, quite literally, contagious.

A curious event at the San Francisco Zoo several years ago reminded me of how easy it is to become entrained to a frenetic rhythm. Six small, sweet, and docile penguins were transferred from Ohio to join forty-six large, fairly lazy, and sometimes ornery penguins at the zoo in San Francisco. As soon as the six were released onto Penguin Island, something changed.

Within two hours, the six Ohio birds somehow convinced the forty-six old-timers not only to join them in the pool but to begin a great migration—to nowhere. Even though the San Francisco birds had never migrated anywhere, the new arrivals persuaded them, within the course of a couple of hours, that this was the way to go.

So for almost three months the fifty-two penguins swam 'round and 'round and 'round, making visitors dizzy. They only came out to sleep for a few hours, then back they went into the pool. Nobody knew when this was all going to stop. Prior to the arrival of the six newcomers, the forty-six penguins could not be coaxed from their homes. "Before, it took a grenade to get them out," said Jane Tollini, their puzzled keeper. As they kept swimming 'round and 'round in circles, Jane joked, "I keep thinking they must be going, 'Didn't we just see that palm tree? Haven't we been here before?'"

The frenzy didn't even stop when the pool was emptied. The penguins simply jumped in and bumped into one another on the dry bottom. Feeding time was, in the keeper's words, hell. "I am kind of like a drive-through restaurant now. They see me, see the fish, run past me, grab the fish, and keep going."

It's easy to laugh at the penguins and the seeming insanity of their pool migration. Yet we can also recognize ourselves and our own tendency to swim swim swim swim swim. How often do we stop and ask ourselves where we are going and why we all seem in such a rush to get there? Are we aware of how we are being entrained by the pace of life around us?

Many moms know they're doing too much, but they don't know how to get out of the pool! They say they'd like to get on another track, but they don't know how. It seems as if everybody else is in this race to somewhere, and it's so easy to get caught up in it. Even our kids are being entrained to the stressful and endless rhythm, and we're beginning to see the cost.

Through practicing Momfulness, we have a chance to help ourselves and our families become just a little bit saner. We experiment with shifting the rhythm of our lives. We practice becoming more mindful of what we are doing and what is driving us. We discover that awareness is often all we need to free ourselves to make other choices. Granted, we don't have as many choices in some areas as we do in others, but my guess is that there are lots of things that we could shift in our families' lives that would slow us down to a healthier and less stressful pace.

As just one example, we might notice a lot of "shoulds" inside our minds that keep us moving in frenetic activity: *I should be a perfect mom. My kids should be involved in lots of extracurricular activities. Birthday parties should be big extravaganzas like everyone else's.* The moment we become curious about these internal messages and observe the power they have over us, they become a little less powerful. And as we begin to experience compassion for ourselves and for others as we race around the pool, perhaps we begin to see another way.

The good news from the story is that it took only six penguins to influence the behavior of the forty-six. Imagine if more and more mothers began to ask, "Is this working for me? Is it working for my children? What societal changes could I help support so that this frenetic pace isn't the norm?" As more and more of us shift into a healthier pace, it is not only our own families who will benefit; it is also society at large.

Relationships Shape Us

Less than five miles away from the penguins at the San Francisco Zoo are three psychiatrists at the UCSF Medical Center: Thomas Lewis, M.D., Fari Amini, M.D., and Richard Lannon, M.D. They have written a book titled *A General Theory of Love,* which draws on the latest research showing that from the time we are born, we are deeply affected by the people close to us. The authors show how our brains link us with the people we love; as a consequence, who we are and who we will become depends, in large measure, on who we love. In a process of entrainment, our brains connect with our loved ones in a rhythm that shapes and changes the very structure and function of our brains. We also sense each other's emotional state and attune ourselves to that.

Most of our communication with others—over 90 percent— is nonverbal. Do we make eye contact with our families? What tone of voice do we use? Is the timing and intensity of our response in sync with our children's? These nonverbal ways of communication are how we let our children know that we see them, that we understand them, and that we love them. The strength of the attachment we form with our children and the healthy creation of their sense of self depends primarily on this communication system that operates underneath the level of our words. Through the way we attune to our children, we shape their lives and, in turn, they shape ours.

In this modern-day world of machines and technology, the subtle nonverbal signals of human beings are often discounted or overlooked. But because the research is so clear on the importance of our children feeling that we really understand what they're communicating and who they are, even the engineers are getting into the act. One dad in Spain was having a very hard time understanding his baby's constant crying, so he did what seemed logical to him. He invented a machine: a baby cry analyzer.

Previously, I had heard about a machine that helped dog owners interpret their pooches' barks, but a *baby cry analyzer* left my mouth hanging open in disbelief. The machine "listens" to a baby's cry for twenty seconds, taking into account the differences in pitch, the frequency of crying spells, and the changes in volume. Then, voilà! A light appears under one of five little faces, indicating whether the baby is experiencing hunger, boredom, discomfort, sleepiness, or stress. When used in conjunction with the accompanying symptoms chart, it claims a success rate of 98 percent. The parent then knows how to respond.

Wow!

I'm really supportive of parents learning to read their children's emotional signals so that they can experience attunement, but I'm curious: What if the buyers of these machines spent those twenty-second interludes learning, instead, to analyze or understand what's happening inside them and their child? What if they discovered that they could trust themselves rather than a machine to listen, learn, make mistakes, and respond to their child in an attuned manner?

It is important to remember that we will never respond perfectly (with or without a machine!) every time our children need us. Often it is hard to make sense of a baby's signals, or we are just too tired to be able to listen. Children are amazingly resilient; we can be "good enough" parents, and when a disconnection or a lack of attunement occurs, we can work to repair it as quickly as possible.

The information about how a child's sense of self is shaped and how a child's brain gets wired, particularly in the early years, is vital in helping us make choices about how we care for our children. (It also underscores why it is crucial for our society to ensure that all parents who work have access to quality caregivers who can provide adequate mirroring to infants and children.)

As we understand such processes as entrainment and attunement, we begin to realize what a positive impact a mother who is mindful, compassionate, and fully present can have on her child's development. If we are constantly stressed, we will find it hard enough to soothe ourselves, let alone our little ones. If we lack flexibility and are rigid in our own predetermined thoughts or ideas about what our child needs, it will be easy to miss what our child is really communicating.

Throughout this book, we will practice entraining to a healthier rhythm. We will increase our ability to attune both to ourselves and to what we need, as well as attend even more deeply to what our children need. Let's turn now to some guidelines for the practice of Momfulness.

Developing a Practice

Motherhood, as I wrote earlier, stretches us in so many ways. It expands us beyond what we think we can do, transforming us in the process. Like many spiritual practices, it teaches us profound lessons. In the rest of this book we will focus on some of these lessons: presence, attention, compassion, embodiment, the sacred in all things, and community.

Within each of the chapters are meditations consisting of essays, observations, or stories. Following each reflective piece is a suggested practice. In designing the practices, I wanted to make sure that they would be easy to do in a short period without a lot of preparation. Most of these practices will weave through your daily routines, not requiring anything but conscious attention. You'll learn that you can apply the practice of Momfulness right where you are—with the family you have, the home you live in, the work you do, the relationships you're in, the religious tradition you grew up with or have chosen.

In this book I make reference to a variety of spiritual traditions. All of us moms, no matter what our religious background, experience both joys and challenges in our lives. As Ariel Gore writes in *The Mother Trip*, "Whatever traditions our faith is rooted in, I know very few mothers who do not pray, at least in secret." We enrich one another when we share what gives us strength, and I have learned so much about my own tradition through studying other faiths. I encourage you to be open-minded and try new practices, shaping them with words and concepts that are meaningful to you.

Our perceptions about what constitutes spiritual practice might need to shift a bit. We might hold preconceived ideas about where to pray, how to meditate, what's supposed to happen, or what holiness looks like. In practicing Momfulness, we are much more likely to find ourselves meditating in a minivan than in a monastery! The delightful discovery we make, as we do these practices, is that there are innumerable sacred moments in our everyday family lives. We don't have to go anywhere else to find holy ground.

The examples and practices in Momfulness come from a number of sources, including the workshops and seminars that I have led over the years, my clinical practice as a psychotherapist, and, most important, my own experience of being a mother. I have witnessed women who felt completely overwhelmed (and that includes all of us at many moments) develop flexibility and the ability to hold in their hearts more than they ever thought they could. One mother wrote to me, "Thank you so much! I have found tools for living my life with my family that I didn't know I had." These tools are within each of us, and we need to keep reminding one another that we can do this.

In terms of the specific practices, remember: *reading about a practice is not the same as doing it.* Think of this book as one you'll experience rather than just read. Play with the practices. Put them into words that make sense to you; adapt them to fit your own religious tradition. Before you rule out doing a practice, you might want to suspend judgment and start from a place of not knowing: What might I discover? What if I tried doing this just for a day? See if you can discover things that delight you, that are interesting to you, that nurture you.

Observe yourself, and watch over the weeks as your body changes, as your mind calms, as your spirit and heart open, and as you feel more connected. You'll be getting to know yourself in a way that's friendly and compassionate. You'll be getting back in touch with your senses. Sometimes you'll feel resistance, and that's OK. Other times you'll feel bliss. Relax into what Momfulness wants you to learn. Be gentle with yourself, and take it at your own pace. Just keep practicing, recognizing that practice doesn't make perfect. Practice is just practice.

One final note: Motherhood is a team sport. While you can go through this book on your own, I recommend finding one friend or e-mail partner you can talk with about what you're doing. Or start a Momfulness group. Come up with your own practices, support each other in your efforts, laugh, and keep one another sane.

Presence

As mothers, our greatest gift to our family is our true presence. We may run around doing many things for them, but it is our *being* that makes all the difference.

To live in the present moment is not easy, as we whirl through life balancing many things at once. As we practice Momfulness, we can pay attention to the moment we are in, finding the wholeness that exists below the busyness. We can come home—to ourselves, to our children, to our partner, to the many extraordinary moments in our everyday family life.

In this chapter we practice being here, now. We relax into life and stop wanting to be somewhere other than where we are. We realize that our true home is so close to us: it is in this moment; it is in the eyes of our child or in the greeting of our partner or in the hug of a dear friend. Our home is as close as our next breath.

May we be fully present, here and now, aware of the gift of each moment.

Breathing Meditation

To breathe is to inhale spirit.

—Huston Smith, *The Soul of Christianity*

One day I received a call from Debby—a mother of three young girls. She had taken one of my workshops. "I want to share with you a story about the breathing prayer you gave us," she began. She was referring to a small card I had handed out that had a simple meditation on it.

"I wanted to remember to breathe while driving the kids around, so I taped one of the cards to the dashboard of my van. My husband, who describes himself as a nonbeliever in what he calls New Age Foo-Foo, teased me about it."

"'*A card to remind you to breathe?*' he asked me." Debby laughed.

"But then one day, our daughters had to go with some friends to Chuck E. Cheese Pizza, and I had another appointment. So I asked my husband to take the kids in my van.

"Four hours later, he returned. He came up to me and said, 'You know that breathing card you have on the dashboard?'

"*Yeeesss,*" I said.

"'Well, *not* that it worked or anything, but let's just say that without it, the kids would never have made it to Chuck E. Cheese!'"

What was on the small card was a simple breathing meditation by the Vietnamese Buddhist monk, Thich Nhat Hanh. It is a two-breath meditation:

Breathing in, I calm my body.
Breathing out, I smile.
Dwelling in the present moment,
I know this is a wonderful moment.

I've found it to be a great way to return to the present moment and reconnect my body and my mind.

Breathing in, I calm my body. When we breathe in and say these words to calm our bodies, we become aware that we even *have* a body. As mothers, it's so easy for us to live in our heads or to be so busy that we forget to tune in to what our bodies need. When we breathe in and give our bodies permission to become calm, our shoulders relax and our stress level begins to decrease.

Breathing out, I smile. This is such a simple instruction, yet the result is so effective. This is not about faking happiness or covering up what we're really feeling. It is about finding the smile that exists in the most ordinary of moments. It is discovering that even when things are crazy—the kids are totally out of control, coworkers are completely unmanageable, traffic is backed up for miles—a part of us remembers that we can smile. It is as if a tiny gap appears between what's happening and the part of us that can observe it all—and smile.

Dwelling in the present moment. As we take this second breath, we recognize how much we live life in the past or in the future. It's as if a tape recording continuously replays what happened or anticipates what might happen. When we push the pause button, take a breath, and dwell in the present moment, we become aware that this really is the only moment that exists. All future moments are only more present moments.

I know this is a wonderful moment. These words help us appreciate how a moment that seems ordinary is actually full of wonder. Suddenly, we have new appreciation for what is right in front of us: the way the sun is coming through the window, the laughter of our children, even the dishes in our kitchen sink. Most moments, if we truly connect to ourselves and to those moments, are wonderful. If it feels like too much to say a moment is wonderful, we can say: *I know this is the* only *moment.* That is always true.

When we use this practice, we discover that underneath it all, supporting us in every moment, is our breath. In and out. In and out. Our breath is with us from the first moment we leave the womb, and it will be with us until we leave this life. In the in-between time, even though we ignore it most of the time, it is there waiting for us to befriend it and to use it as a way of coming home.

Breathing can also be a prayer—a way of connecting to God, to the Sacred, and to our deepest self. The words *breath* and *spirit* come from the same root word in a number of languages, and most religious traditions have some form of breathing meditation or prayer. When we link our breath to the power of Spirit, using words or phrases that feel sacred, we open up a channel of healing and wholeness that is available to us in any moment.

When I sit to pray or meditate, I begin by using my breath, recalling the unity of breath and Spirit. I've taught this practice to my children, and they each have their own favorite version. They tell me it helps them deal with the stresses of school and the times when they feel nervous or anxious. We often begin bedtime prayer with a breathing meditation, and at our church we open Sunday school by lighting a candle in the center of the circle and breathing in and out God's love.

Recently, Debby called me again to tell me a second story about the power of the breathing prayer. "My five-year-old daughter developed a tumor in her throat. I can't tell you how many times I used the breathing prayer every day. That was all I could do, just breathe, pray, and stay in that moment."

Debby went on to tell me how she taught her little girl how to breathe and smile in order to calm herself through all the poking and prodding that the doctors were doing to her. "We also did the breathing prayer together every night, and it helped my little angel fall asleep.

"It's amazing," Debby continued. "Through all of this, as painful as it's been, I've discovered that our entire community was ready to help my family, and this has been a great gift. We've each felt held in a loving connection to God, to one another, to our friends and families—even to strangers."

After her daughter underwent surgery to remove the tumor, the surgeon came out to speak to Debby. "I don't know what you told your daughter, but whatever it was, she was amazing. She was so calm and peaceful; everything went beautifully, much better than I expected," he said.

In the weeks that they had to wait for the final biopsy report to come back with the good news that the tumor was benign, Debby and her daughter often did a breathing meditation together. "I'd start feeling anxious, and then I'd breathe in and out and pray. In the midst of all of this, I really felt that each of these moments was a wonderful moment."

See if you can make Breathing Meditation a daily practice. You might want to make cards to remind you to breathe consciously, writing down phrases that help you connect mind with body, breath with spirit. Use it as a prayer, as a way of coming home to the wonder of each moment.

Sacred World Practice
Breathing Meditation

Try it now: take a breath in and say to yourself, *Breathing in, I calm my body.*

- On the out breath say, *Breathing out, I smile.*
- Repeat these phrases as you breathe in and out a few times.
- As you do this, notice what happens.
  How do your shoulders feel? Your stomach? Your face?
  Did your smile come easily?
- Now take some breaths in and out while you say to yourself,
  Dwelling in the present moment, I know this is a wonderful moment.
  Are you at home in this moment?
  Are you aware of the wonder in this ordinary moment?
- Just notice whatever happens, even resistance.
- No judgment. Just breathing in and out.

I See Me in Your Eyes

To discover God, make a lap.

—David Spangler, *Parent as Mystic, Mystic as Parent*

"Mama, can we sit in Happy and snuggle?" my eight-year-old daughter asked.

("Happy" is the name Julianna gave to the rocking chair where I used to nurse her when she was little. We've been calling it that for years, ever since the day when, instead of making the clicking sound she usually made when she wanted to nurse, she pointed to the chair and said, "Happy?" Even at a year and a half, she knew that what went on in that chair had a lot to do with being happy.)

I looked at my watch. "Honey, I'm running a little late. I'm getting ready to go give a talk about connection," I told her.

Her lip went out in a pout. Then I recognized the irony of my statement. I looked again at my watch and did a quick calculation.

"OK, sweetie. I have a few minutes. Let's snuggle."

Her face beamed. We sat in Happy, and she lay across my lap. We rocked back and forth, back and forth, looking at each other, smiling and content. A few minutes later an expression of delight crossed her face.

"Mama," she said with amazement. "I see *me* in your eyes." She could literally see herself reflected in my eyes. I stopped rocking, and then I saw myself in her eyes.

꠸

We may not realize it, but we often go through an entire day without really making eye contact with our family. We talk to our children with our backs turned or while checking e-mail or in the car. Many moms pride themselves on their ability to multitask, and I'm no exception. But if we ask our kids whether we're as good at this as we think we are, we might be surprised. One day my son Matt, who was thirteen at the time, was talking to me while I was reading the newspaper. Earlier I had bragged to him about my juggling-many-things-at-once expertise, and he didn't say anything. At this moment, however, he felt completely frustrated with my lack of attention.

"I've decided you *can* do two things at once," he said loudly. "You're just lousy at both of them!"

This state of being present in body but not in mind or heart is called *absent presence* and is actually the state that most of us live in much of the time. It's as if we are walking ghosts. Our children know that we're not really there. They don't feel truly seen or heard by us. Love is a body-to-body experience; when we don't make real contact, our loved ones don't experience the fullness of love. And neither do we.

I heard it said once, "God comes through the eyes." When we drop into that place of presence, we truly can see one another in our reflections. We don't need lots of time to do this; a moment in which we are fully present is all that is required. In that moment, we come home.

Eye Contact Meditation

As you go through your day today, notice whether you make eye contact with your children.

- One or two times today, when your children want to talk with you, stop what you're doing, turn toward them, and make eye contact with them.
- Move out of "absent presence" and take a breath to become fully present, bringing your mind and body together.
- Hold your gaze a few seconds longer than you normally would.
- Notice how it feels inside you.
- Notice how your child responds.
- See if you can send love through your eyes.

Remember: from a biological point of view, when you look at someone's eyes and make an emotional connection, both of you experience a greater sense of well-being, and your physical health is enhanced.

Rolling Hippo Meditation

When we are too busy doing things for our children,
we forget how important it is to simply be with them.
—Daniel Siegel and Mary Hartzell, *Parenting from the Inside Out*

Sometimes we find spiritual teachers in the most unexpected of places. I found one of mine on one of what the Dalai Lama calls "those wonderful nature programs" on TV. (I was happy to discover that, like me, he enjoys watching animal documentaries just before bed.)

It was at the end of one of those "what's-it-all-about-Alfie?" days, when I had wondered all day whether my sole purpose in

life *really was* to pick up dirty socks, that I curled up on my pillow
and turned on a documentary on hippopotami. I watched, mes-
merized. These big lugs really are quite beautiful!

The mama hippo stands neck deep in the river while her
baby rolls its barrel-body around and around in the water. The
little hippo spins in these circles next to its mom for five, ten,
maybe twenty complete rotations. Mom just stands there with a
big hippo grin. Every once in a while she takes a really deep
breath and then submerges and lies on the river bottom for five
or six minutes so that her baby can nurse. That's how they spend
their days: roll, nurse, roll, nurse.

As I watched this, I realized that I have a very hard time
doing nothing but watch my baby hippo spin. If I'm not doing
something that I label "productive," I get anxious. I also get bored.
To sit on the floor with my child for an extended amount of time
is one of the most challenging things I can do. My body may be
doing floor time, but my head is racing through my to-do lists,
not even present in the room.

What helps me relax into my "mama animal" self is to understand what is happening inside me and inside my child. In terms
of my own brain, it's normal that it gets restless. Human beings

are wired to seek out novelty. Knowing that, I can use these times to practice mindfulness, returning to the present moment when my thoughts drift away. I can take a breath, smile, reconnect my mind with my body, returning to this moment with my child. Over and over again, this is the practice.

In terms of my baby's brain, an incredible process is happening as we sit together on the floor. Millions of new synapses (the wiring that connects the neurons) are being laid down each second. These connections get strengthened when there is a rich environment and sufficient stimulation. When I touch and hold and talk with and sing to and play with my baby, I'm literally helping shape my child—in body and soul.

And so, right now, when my baby hippo needs hang-out time, we practice Rolling Hippo Meditation: roll, sit, snuggle, roll, sit, snuggle.

Watching Your Children Play

This is a practice of simply watching your children while they are playing.

- Don't intrude into their play; just let them be.
- Watch. Listen.
- Move away from your idea about who they are or should be, and notice who they really are.
  What are their gifts?
  What do they love?
- Watch their faces as their eyes light up or they smile.
- Watch as they scowl.
- Listen to the sound of their laughter or their conversation.
- Imagine how they see the world.
- See them for the unique souls they are.

How a Mom Prays

I have stilled and quieted
my soul like a weaned child,
Like a weaned child on its mother's lap,
so is my soul within me.
—Psalm 131

One morning, when I was nine months pregnant with my
first child, I was sitting in a rocking chair praying the "Our Father."
As I began the prayer, I felt my baby kick; in that moment, the
word *our* took on a new reality. It moved me from being an
individual "I" into a collective "we." From that time forward,
I have often prayed while holding my children.

Here is a translation of a lovely poem by a fifteenth-century Indian poet, Kabir, which I've used as a prayer while holding a child:

Inside this clay jug there are canyons and pine mountains,
and the maker of canyons and pine mountains!
All seven oceans are inside, and hundreds of millions
    of stars.
The acid that tests gold is there, and the one who judges
    jewels.
And the music from the strings that no one touches,
and the source of all water.
If you want the truth, I will tell you the truth:
Friend, listen: the God whom I love is inside.
    —Robert Bly, *The Kabir Book*

As I wrap my arms around the "clay jug" of my child, I am in awe. I am mother to a universe. I look into my child's eyes, pools that go on forever. I hear an invitation: *Come home. Remember who you are, who your children are.*

We are all clay jugs filled with God; we are beings overflowing with stars and with the source of all water: living water, still water, rolling water, water with salt, water with tears. Creation and Creator reside in that which we hold.

We won't hear this on television or on talk radio; we won't read it in the newspaper. In the busyness and the technology of our modern world, in Creation that we cement over or wall off, it is easy to lose touch with ourselves, with the wild beauty that is us. It is easier, perhaps, to get glimpses of this original beauty in our children; they can help us remember that we, too, hold the universe.

If we are to recognize this, and if our children are to recognize it, we must create the space of remembering, of looking deeply, of being present to the sacred that we hold in our arms and in our hearts.

Presence Practice

Invite someone—your spouse, a friend, a family member—to join you in this practice.

- ℘ Place your hand on the other person's back.
- ℘ Hold the intention (decide) that you are going to be fully present to this other person, right now.

- Don't talk. Just be present, with your hand on your partner's back.
- Do this for about two minutes.
- Now withdraw your intention to be present. Leave your hand on the other person's back, but put your mind elsewhere. *What's for dinner tonight? Are the dishes done?*
- Intentionally put your body and your mind in two different places.
- Do this for about one minute.
- Finally, return to your partner; intend again to be fully present.
- Feel your hand on the other's back.
- After another minute, stop and share with each other what the experience was like.
- If there's time, change places, and let the other person have the chance to be intentionally present and intentionally absent.
- Then practice being present with your children as you make a lap and hold the universe in your arms.

The Alone Hat

It is a difficult lesson to learn today—to leave one's friends
and family and deliberately practice the art of solitude for
an hour or a day or a week.
—Anne Morrow Lindbergh, *Gift from the Sea*

As mothers, we go through life at breakneck speed,
bombarded with noise and with the needs of others. We are
responsible for an endless assortment of tasks: scheduling
orthodontic appointments, figuring out what's for dinner,
remembering what weekend we signed up to bring the school
guinea pig home, breaking up sibling fights, getting the tires
rotated, wiping noses and fingers and bottoms. It's hard to hear
ourselves think, let alone remember that we are breathing.

Our spirits long for a time out, for a few moments of peace and quiet. That's why I think that something my daughter Julianna made when she was three years old is so brilliant. It's an Alone Hat. (She got the idea from a cartoon show.) My sister loved it so much she thought it was worthy of the Nobel Prize!

Here's how it came about. One day Julianna jumped off the coffee table; after her dad told her not to do that, she ran up to her room and shut the door. A few minutes later, she returned carrying a large sheet of paper on which she had scribbled lots of angry-looking black marks. She scowled at her dad as she brought me the paper and a stapler.

"Mama, will you staple this into a cone shape?" she asked me. After I did so, she walked out of the room. When she reappeared, she was wearing the large, dunce-like cone on her head. It covered her eyes, ears, and mouth.

"Hummmph!" she huffed, hoping we heard her. "*This* is my Alone Hat. When I'm wearing this, I can't hear you or see you. Hummmph!"

"Do you want to tell us what you're feeling?" we asked. (We're not psychotherapists for nothing!)

"I can't heeaaarrr you," she called out. Then she humphed again, turned, and with the cone head in place, slowly zig-zagged across the kitchen, bumping into every chair and wall in her path.

She eventually got over her anger and left the hat on the table. A few hours later my sister Nancy came over to visit and saw the hat. "What's this?" Nancy asked.

"Ah," I said. "*That* is an Alone Hat." She decided to try it on. The large cone covered her ears and eyes, and she found herself in her own little world. "This is fabulous!" Nancy shouted through the paper. "I think you could market these to moms across America. It would be like a signal to our husbands and children to let us have a little peace and quiet!"

It took a while for Nancy to relinquish the hat.

ॐ

What if we mothers (figuratively) donned our Alone Hats for a few moments each day and created little zones of quiet where we could get in touch again with ourselves? We'd be less frazzled, less depleted, less confused about what we're doing and why we're doing it. Taking care of ourselves—body, mind, and spirit— is a gift we give to our families as well as to ourselves.

Parker Palmer, in his book *Let Your Life Speak,* writes:

[S]elf-care is never a selfish act—it is simply good stewardship of the only gift I have, the gift I was put on earth to offer
to others. Anytime we can listen to true self and give it the
care it requires, we do so not only for ourselves but for
the many others whose lives we touch.

The fact is that we are much better parents and partners
and friends when we make a commitment of time and effort to
strengthen the spiritual core within us. We may make excuses
that we don't have a few minutes to do this, but we usually
manage to get the kids to swimming lessons and ourselves to
hair appointments.

So today, take a few moments and put on your Alone Hat.
Create a quiet space where silence, grace, and peace can nurture
your spirit.

Alone Hat Practice

Today, take some alone time. Even if it's only five minutes.

- Do the equivalent of putting on an Alone Hat.
- Light a candle. Go for a walk. Sit outside.
- Lock yourself in the bathroom.
- Create a little zone of quiet.
- Congratulate yourself for taking this time. It's an act of love.
- Now imagine that your life is like an ocean.
- At the surface, there can also be a lot of turbulence. Life's busyness and demands and ups and downs can be like rough waves that whirl around us.
- Now imagine that deep down in the ocean, thirty or forty feet below the surface, is a place of constant stillness.
- Take a breath, and drop down into this place of quiet and calm.

As you keep practicing this in your alone moments, it'll get easier to practice in the midst of the chaos of a day. You'll discover that you can drop into that place of stillness wherever you are.

Porch Swing

Time stands still best
in moments that look suspiciously
like ordinary life.
—Brian Andreas, *Trusting Soul*

Mama, I love this place."

My young daughter nestles close beside me as we rock
back and forth, back and forth, on the old porch swing. The
freshly painted yellow house, with its green and white trim, is
the perfect backdrop on this beautiful spring day. The wooden
boards beneath our feet creak with our gentle movement.

Here we have room enough for life. We have a rhythm to our day. We have exactly enough time for what is truly important.

I wonder: Does the fact that we happen to be sitting on a swing that is part of a museum display say something about the pace of life today?

ℰ

Today was a work and school holiday, and rather than stay home and check items off of my to-do list, I decided to spend some quality time with my daughter, Julianna. We headed to the Children's Discovery Museum—a bustling place where children busily explore many aspects of the world. There are displays that demonstrate how electricity works and exhibits where kids can blow huge bubbles and pour thousands of seeds. There is a real ambulance and a fire truck that they can climb into and traffic lights that children can operate.

Julianna enjoys all these displays. But her favorite is the one with the porch swing, titled "Step Into the Past." The museum has created a reproduction of what life was like in Silicon Valley, where we live. Decades ago it was known as "The Valley of Heart's Delight," and eight million fruit and nut trees grew here in the most fertile soil on earth. Now concrete covers much of the land, and most of what we know of orchards is from photographs like the large ones lining the wall of this museum.

In this replica of life from the past, there is an old grindstone; there are rusty tools hanging on a barn wall and an antique telephone switchboard where children can plug in wires and have pretend conversations. Over in the corner there is an early animation apparatus: it is a horizontal wheel with tiny slits that you spin and then peek through in order to see sequential drawings of a horse trotting. As you look through the rotating openings, there is an illusion of movement.

As my daughter and I sit on the porch, a harried mother comes rushing by, moving quickly from object to object. She stands over the wheel and spins it, not sure what it is supposed to do. She looks at me and says with exasperation, "It's broken. Everything in here is broken." What she doesn't know is that she must squat down to a child's level and look through the little openings in order to see the magic.

On another day that mother might have been me. But this porch swing has shifted something inside me and transported me to a quiet and peaceful place. As I reflect on all the changes of the last century, I'm not sure what it all means. I know we can't go back. And certainly there are parts of the past that I wouldn't want to return to, like the old wringer washer and scrub board that children are playing with as we sit and rock.

Yet I can't help but think that something important is being lost. In the name of development, we cover the earth with concrete and then wonder why we feel heavier inside. Our hearts feel a little more closed, not quite as soft as they used to be. While we need freeways to get around, we spend so much time on them that it's no wonder it's hard to slow down in our personal lives. Perhaps without the equivalent of porch swings, we lose a vital perspective on the world.

My daughter doesn't seem to care that the yellow house we're sitting in front of is really just a façade or that we're rocking on the equivalent of a movie set. To her, even if the porch is not real, her mother making time to snuggle next to her *is* real, and that is all that matters.

After a while, we return home; when we arrive, I stand on our tiny porch, wondering if it could hold a swing. But then I realize that what I long for is not to step back into simpler times. I want to step fully into the present. I want to slow down, to sit and snuggle, to nurture and care for the beauty that is around us right now. I want to be fully present to those I love and be grateful for each moment.

Ordinary Moment Meditation

Mother Teresa is credited with saying:

> Everybody today seems to be in such a terrible rush, anxious for greater developments and greater riches and so on, so that children have very little time for their parents. Parents have very little time for each other, and in the home begins the disruption of the peace of the world.

- This week, spend some "ordinary time" with one child.
- Do something relaxed together; take time together that's not rushed.
- Pick your child up for lunch and go on a picnic.
- Make a tent with blankets and read a book in it together.
- Go to a park and swing.
- Sit and snuggle on a front porch.

Know that this practice benefits *both* of you. Your bodies slow down and entrain to a healthier pace, your busy minds relax, and you become more fully present to yourselves and to each other.

Attention

*O*ur minds are so busy. If we listen carefully, we can hear our constant inner dialogue with ourselves. Every day we're making up stories about our lives, we're making judgments about ourselves or other people, we're telling ourselves that life will be better when X, Y, or Z happens, and we get impatient for that future moment. Sometimes we even think that "real life" is not the life we're living.

The way we talk to ourselves influences the way we parent. So often we don't understand what our child is expressing because we're caught up in our own thoughts or feelings. As we practice Momfulness, we become curious about all this, and we develop the capacity to pay attention to and observe our minds. We notice how we miss what's really happening because of our own, more limited, ideas about what's happening. We see how we generate much of our own suffering through what we tell ourselves or through our desire to have things be different from how they are now. In this chapter we practice treating ourselves with gentleness and humor.

May we pay attention with kindness to what is happening within us and within our children.

Plan B

We can proceed according to the planned itinerary,
strenuously trying to make life conform to our needs, or
we can adapt to whatever we meet and flow without effort.
—Piero Ferrucci, *What Our Children Teach Us*

Today I make a short visit to the park near my daughter's
school. I stand at the edge of a small stream and listen to the
sound of water flowing over rocks. As I turn to leave, I feel a
pull inside, a whisper: *Not yet, there's something more to see.*
Look closer.

I step over tree roots, closer to the water. I squint, as if that can help me see better. *I must be fooling myself, there's nothing else here.* And then I notice a movement out of the corner of my left eye, downstream just a bit.

It is a family of ducks: a coffee-brown mother, an emerald-headed father, and seven brand-new ducklings. The mother steps out on the opposite bank, and the huddled mass of babies follows. The male duck waits in the stream. He is a sentinel; his eyes never leave me.

Mama duck waddles over the large roots. I can no longer see the little ones. Then one-by-one, they pop up over the top of the tree roots, not wanting to let their protector get out of their sight. I count—4, 5, 6. One is missing. I hold my breath. The mother pauses as she feels the absence of one. After an endless minute, number 7 leaps up and joins its siblings.

The mother duck waddles back into the stream, to the place where the water rushes over rocks in a whitewater cascade. She's decided to swim upstream and take her brood with her.

The seven ducklings attempt to follow her. They are paddling as hard as they can, but they are making no forward progress. The water carries them ever backwards. They begin to peep, and it is not the sound of delight in their cries. *We can't do this.* They let mom know that they are doing all they can, and it's not enough; she's going beyond where they can go.

As I watch, I witness a moment of grace. The mother stops paddling her feet, and she simply lets go. She recognizes that this isn't working for today. Her little ones aren't quite ready for this journey. So she simply turns and lets the water carry her down the rapids and into the calm waters below.

The ducklings stop their cries. The magnificent seven follow their mother—kids on a waterslide, bobbing and riding down whitewater. They look like they're enjoying it, and I can almost hear them yell, "Again! Again!" They float over to the side of the creek, and a few minutes later, they are fast asleep.

ᴖ

Life rushes under all of us; although there are times when it's necessary for us to swim upstream and *not* go with the flow, there are many more times when the grace lies in simply letting go.

My trouble is that I think there is a track that things should stay on. I'm hooked to a belief that life *should* go a certain way.

I develop an attachment to a Plan A and set up my expectations accordingly.

An important part of spiritual practice is to learn to let go, to recognize that Plan A exists only in my head. When I find myself irritated by changes in my schedule or resisting whatever is happening around me, I tell myself, *We're now in Plan B.* In fact, it's become a daily mantra: *Life as Plan B.* It makes it much easier for me to relax and surrender to the moment.

With my children, I've noticed how there are days when I'm asking them (and myself!) to go too far, too soon—to paddle too furiously upstream. I press on, but for what? To get to the next place? *Hurry up. Hurry up. Come on. Let's go.* At those times, I don't experience the joy of the rapids, of going with the flow. I fight what *is* rather than relaxing into it.

So for today, I'm taking a lesson from this mother duck. I let go and let grace carry me home.

Plan B Practice

What happens when life doesn't go the way you planned?

Did the babysitter cancel this morning?

Is your child sick and having to stay home from school?

Are you running late?

Is your summer going differently from the way you had planned?

Does your mom or dad require unexpected medical care?

When things like this occur, can you just be with whatever is happening?

Notice if you are telling yourself things like this: *It's not fair. This shouldn't be happening. This is terrible, horrible, catastrophic. Why me?*

- Take a breath.
- Experience how things *are* going rather than how you want them to go.
- Take another breath.
- Tell yourself: *I'd prefer not to have to deal with this, but this is what's happening, and I can handle it.*
- Say to yourself, *We're in Plan B now.* (Or Plan C or D or Q!)
- Recognize that Plan A usually only exists in our heads.

Autopilot

Fortunately analysis is not the only way to resolve inner conflicts. Life itself still remains a very effective therapist.
—Karen Horney, *Our Inner Conflicts*

If you asked my sons for a phrase to put on my tombstone, I bet it would read, "Be Careful."

To be honest, I just realized this yesterday. I was on the phone with my twenty-one-year-old son Matt. At the end of a nice conversation, I said, "Be careful." It just came out.

"Mom, I'm *shopping*. What do you mean, be careful?" he joked. I found out later that he was Christmas shopping with his stepmother at the mall. Oops.

With a sudden recognition, I realize that I've been saying that phrase since my first child was born. "Be careful," I'd say to anyone who held my new baby. When he was learning to walk, I'd say it to him. When he was a toddler and climbed up the slide at the playground, out it came: "Be careful." Again and again, through four kids and twenty-five years, I keep adding my two-cent warning. Whether they're walking to school, playing soccer, playing baseball, walking around the block, riding a bike, driving a car, snowboarding down a mountain—you name it, I'm there with my caution.

I say that I want to live my life, and I want my kids to live theirs, in a way that's large and free and fully alive. But the reality is a bit different: all this worrying and fretting is constricting and exhausting. It's not that "Be careful" is a *bad* phrase. It's just such a protective-mom phrase. Perhaps it has come in handy and done its job a few times, but mostly I'm on autopilot and say it out of a habit of fear.

I learned early in my life to do worst-case-scenario thinking. I'm a pro. I figured if I imagined all the things that could go wrong, in gory detail, that I was preparing myself to handle them. Instead, it gave me stomach knots and insomnia. I inherited this worrying from my mother, and she inherited it from her mother. I haven't noticed too much of it in my sons, but my daughter is beginning to shout to her brothers, "Drive carefully," as they leave home for their own apartments.

It doesn't help that fear seems to be all around us; many of us today are living more pinched-face with worry, worry, worry. We watch the news, and it can make us crazy. *Give children lots of salmon to eat. Wait, don't. It has too many chemicals! It's OK for pregnant women to drink coffee. Oops, no it's not!* Even simple decisions can become difficult: Is it safe for our kids to walk to school? Can they play in the front yard? It's easy to see how fear can become our constant companion.

This way of living is not healthy for children or other living things, including mothers! By becoming mindful of what we are telling ourselves and of how we are increasing our own level of fear, we can begin to make different choices.

Changing this habit is not going to be easy. I've already caught myself saying, "Be careful!" once today. But I've also stopped myself—twice.

There is a lot of power in the words we use. If I want to step out of fear and into a healthy and wise relaxation with life, then shifting what I say can help. I've discovered that sending my children off with a "Have fun!" gives *me* much more energy, and it brings a smile to their faces. And in the end, I'd much rather have those words on my tombstone!

Becoming Mindful of Our Phrases

Author Brenda Ueland (in *If You Want to Write*) playfully suggests that parents become more conscious of how they talk with their children:

> Don't ask your poor children those automatic questions—"Did you wash your hands, dear?"—those dull, automatic, querulous, duty questions (almost the only conversation that most parents have to offer). Note the look of dreadful exhaustion and ennui and boredom that comes into their otherwise quite happy faces.

Begin to notice, without judgment, how you talk with your kids or your spouse.

- Just notice if you're on automatic pilot.
- Become aware of your favorite phrases:
  "Who made this mess?"
  "I'm not your maid!"

"Get your feet off the table!"

"Clean your room."

"Be careful."

"Turn the TV down!"

"Just wait 'til *you* have kids."

"I don't care what your friends get to do; I say No."

"Don't slam the door!"

"Don't play ball in the house!"

Do these reactions stem from anxiety? boredom? caretaking? Are they messages you grew up with in your own childhood?

- Don't make any judgments; just observe yourself.
  Wow, I said that one again!
- When you catch yourself about to say one of these, try an experiment. Keep quiet. Notice if it's easy or hard to not say anything.
- You can also experiment with saying something completely silly or unexpected and enjoy the reaction of your family members when you do.

The River

Everything is connected; everything changes; pay attention.
—Jane Hirshfield

My sister Nancy called yesterday in tears. "What's wrong?"
I asked.

"Nothing. It's just that I had an experience last night that made me cry. I'm not really sad; I just had this recognition about life. I'm teaching the book *Siddhartha* to my high school kids, and I think it's affecting me."

Nancy is a high school English teacher who is passionate about her work. She is also the mother of two girls—Christine, age fourteen, and Amelia, age ten. "Here," she said, "let me read you a passage from the book. It's about how there really is no such thing as time."

> But today he only saw one of the river's secrets, one that gripped his soul. He saw that the water continually flowed and flowed and yet it was always there; it was always the same and yet every moment it was new. Who could understand, conceive this? He did not understand it; he was only aware of a dim suspicion, a faint memory, divine voices. [Herman Hesse, *Siddhartha*]

"Anyway," Nancy went on, "last night I was chaperoning at the eighth-grade graduation dinner, and Christine and the other seventh graders were helping. They showed a slide presentation of the kids who were graduating, beginning when they were in kindergarten, and suddenly I had a *Siddhartha* moment. It was like I was looking into the river.

"I saw Christine as she is now, in seventh grade, and I saw the faces of the eighth graders and the pictures of the kindergartners, and realized they're all connected. Next year Christine would be sitting here as a graduate watching the slideshow of her younger self, and I suddenly saw Amelia as a kindergartner and third grader and eighth grader all simultaneously, and the pictures of all the families looked just like all of ours."

Nancy took a deep breath. "I had a realization of the endless stream that life is, and that we are all part of it, and that it just keeps continually flowing, and when we look at it, like at a stream, there is always just the present, this moment."

She laughed a bit between her tears. "Then today in class I shared what I had felt the night before and related it to the book, and one of the boys in class teased me. I started crying, and all the other kids were sweet and tried to comfort me. I feel kind of stupid—but I did get their attention!"

I told her I understood and that I've had many of those moments with my children as they've grown. This year, during the Halloween parade at my daughter's school, I cried, not so much because I was sad but more because I recognized the preciousness of a moment. For each of the last six years, I had dressed Julianna in a Halloween costume, and each year she sat with her class on the playground in the designated spot for her grade level. When she was in kindergarten, I looked across the playground at where the fifth graders sat; I couldn't imagine my youngest child that big.

But with each passing year Julianna and her classmates moved up, and this year she sat with her fifth-grade class on that once-distant spot. Now it was time to look across the playground at the kindergarteners, and I had a hard time remembering when she was that small. During the parade, the children from every grade processed in front of us with delight, and it felt like the endless stream of life.

As I look deeply at the lives of my children, I see how everything changes and how everything is connected. The river is flowing; it is always there, it is always the same, and yet every moment it is new.

River-of-Life Meditation

In an interview with Elizabeth Lund, of *The Christian Science Monitor,* the poet Jane Hirshfield used seven words to describe the nature of this life: *Everything is connected; everything changes; pay attention.*

She added, "And really, you only need the last two—if you're paying attention, you'll find out whatever else you need to know."

- See how everything is connected and how everything changes.
- Remember back to your childhood, to the little girl that you were.
- What did you love then? What did you want to be when you grew up? What has stayed constant within you? What has changed?
- Think about each of your children.
- Remember their births and their early toddler years.
- Look into the river of their lives.
- Now as you look at them, imagine your own parents as toddlers.
- Move forward in time and imagine your great-grandchildren as they are learning to walk.

In prayer or meditation, you might want to use the phrases: *Everything is connected; everything changes; pay attention.*

Is it possible to notice that eternity exists in this very moment?

Mouth Yoga

Smiling is very important. If we are not able to smile,
then the world will not have peace.
—Thich Nhat Hanh, *Being Peace*

Buddhist monk Thich Nhat Hanh refers to smiling as "mouth yoga," and he believes that smiling can change not only your life— it can change civilization.

When our babies are brand new, we wait and watch and make fools of ourselves trying to coach them in their first smile. When it happens, we smile in return, we laugh, we beam, we run to their baby book and record it (well, only if it's a first child and he or she *has* a baby book). In those early weeks and months, we realize that smiles are small miracles.

Our children's smiles continue to captivate us for a while, but gradually we stop seeing them for the marvel that they are. Have we lost touch with the miracle of our own smile? Smiling is often one of the first things to disappear from our hassled lives. Our face develops grim lines, and we don't realize how stern we always look. Before we know it, we've lost our smile, and the level of happiness in our home changes. Our children see us and wonder if they really want to grow up to be adults that look like they never have much fun.

Smiles need to be stretched and exercised if we want them to get stronger. Mouth yoga makes not only our faces feel better but our whole bodies. When we smile, endorphins are released, and hundreds of muscles in the face and body relax. Our mood is improved, and we begin to care for others with more humor and kindness.

Until you practice it, you won't realize how powerful it can be. Smile when you're doing the dishes, or when you're folding the laundry, or when you're stopped at a red light, or first thing in the morning before you get up. No matter what you are doing, take a deep breath and smile.

Doing mouth yoga won't get the dishes done any faster or create less laundry for us to do. What smiling will do is remind us that underneath all of our busyness, there's grace, there's a spaciousness that we can bring inside of us. It reminds us that in this moment, we are well. Perhaps we'll be surprised to discover ourselves being grateful for the soapy water, for the folded socks, for the noisy kids in the backseat. Perhaps in that moment we will find peace.

Smiling is a wonderful practice to do in families. Maybe it's the end of a long day; you've raced out of work, picked up the kids, managed to put dinner on the table, and plopped into your chair. You're ready to eat. Before you start to gulp down your food and wipe up the kids' spills, spend one moment looking around at your family. Take a deep breath. Now smile.

Smiling can change how you eat your meal. It can mean the difference between your being present and grateful for your family and your feeling burdened or stressed by your family. Your meal together can become nourishing at many levels.

You may feel some resistance to smiling, as you might with any new exercise program. Play with it. Experiment with slight smiles, maybe letting just the corners of your mouth tilt up half a centimeter. Even doing this just once a day, at a time when you don't ordinarily smile, can bring your body and mind together again, and this will help you feel so much better.

As Thich Nhat Hanh tells us, "Simple practices like conscious breathing and smiling are very important. They can change our civilization" (*Peace Is Every Step*). So today, change civilization—or at least change the way you are fully present in this moment. Who knows, maybe they are one and the same!

Mouth Yoga

Right now, practice some mouth yoga.

- ℘ As you read this, smile.

  Is it a little smile?

  Can you make it bigger?

- ℘ Pay attention to how your face feels.

  Do you notice any resistance?

  Do you notice any shifts in your body? Your mind?

- ℘ Take a few breaths while smiling.

- ℘ Later today, see if you can remember to find your smile.

- ℘ Surprise yourself! Find yourself smiling in situations where you'd least expect to.

The Ideal vs. the Real

The real meditative practice is to open up to the full range of what happens in life. And parenting is a fantastic arena for doing that kind of spiritual training. It's as much a potential door into enlightenment as anything else.

—Jon Kabat-Zinn (from an interview in *YES! Magazine,* 1998)

J'm sitting on the second floor of the city library, looking out a huge glass window at Central Park. Our city's park is not nearly as large as New York's, but it is ours. It is a little oasis of green in an area of concrete; its lawns and weeping willows and redwoods release their cool breath into our souls. There is a small man-made lake in the center that has too much algae and smells in the summer, but its water still attracts ducks and seagulls and Canada geese—and toddlers that chase them all.

I came to the library today because my own house seems too noisy and messy, and I am hoping for some sense of order and quiet. Maybe here I can have an uninterrupted thought. Maybe here I can escape everyone's demands. Maybe here I can write a book on mindful mothering without so many kids around.

Sigh.

Down on the grass below the library, I see a bronze statue; it is a life-size rendering of seven children holding hands and dancing in a circle. The three boys and four girls are all smiling. They are all quiet. They are all behaving as perfect friends. They will be doing this for perhaps fifty or sixty years.

The sun is shining off their copper-colored hair. A bird lands on one girl's head. A squirrel is looking for food around one boy's feet.

Such well-mannered children. Such pleasant quiet here in the library. My eyes close, my thoughts drift. I recall that the statue of the children is called "Circle of Peace." Such a lovely concept.

I wonder if the sculptor gathered a group of real children to pose for this piece. I imagine he did, and I picture the scene: well-behaved children, no whining, no fighting—the kind of kids you could take anywhere.

Oops. As I watch the scene in my head, the children start getting antsy. One pulls another down. Now they're all laughing and wrestling. All bets are off. *Wait, kids, get back into your circle of peace!* Too late, they're all running around, chasing each other. The sculptor tries to get control. The children's parents are mortified.

I open my eyes. I'm relieved when I see that the statue is still here, the children are still holding hands, and the grass is still growing under their feet. All is well. But wait. Now a real-life boy, one with blood and flesh and mischief, is walking by the bronze bunch. He's staring them down. After looking around to make sure no one is watching, he gives one of the bronze boys a swift kick in the butt.

Ah yes, the circle of peace.

I laugh as I realize that the natural order has been restored. Children do not play perfectly, and if they did, what would be the fun in that?

These perfect ones, who stand in rain and heat, their smiles unchanging, may be some parents' fantasy. Yet these children of gold, when the sun goes down, are cold. Our own children are breathing and squirmy; they have soft cheeks and warm bodies that we inhale like fresh-baked bread. They are the real deal.

So I'm packing up my laptop now. It's time to go home. It's time to say yes to all of life—the whines and the arguments, the soft kisses, the messy house, the flesh-and-blood kids that are perfect just as they are. It is time to say a big yes to the real things of my life.

Ideal vs. Real Meditation

When you look at your life, do you long for something different? Do you grumble at the mess?

What if you shifted your attitude, just for a moment, and felt grateful that you live in the midst of this family, with all of its stickiness and disorder?

Notice what you feel when real life is not living up to the ideal in your head:

- *This is going to be the perfect Christmas-tree-cutting outing!* (And then the kids fight and Dad ends up yelling and the tree falls off the car roof.)
- *Disneyland is going to be so much fun!* (Of course, the kids whine and are ungrateful and Mickey Mouse scares the baby.)

- Practice being with the real things of your family life.

Clearing Clutter

Getting rid of clutter is not about letting go of things that are meaningful to you. It's about letting go of things that no longer contribute to your life so you have the time and the energy and the space for the things that do.

—Elaine St. James, *Living the Simple Life*

A year ago, I had full-blown writer's block. No matter what I tried, I couldn't seem to get unstuck. Then one night I had a dream that told me that I wouldn't be able to write until I cleared out a certain corner of our living room.

The particular corner in question is one that I face when I sit in my usual writing chair in that room. The next morning, after taking my accustomed seat and trying for twenty minutes to write a coherent thought, I remembered my dream. Even though the corner was a bit messy (there was a small stereo, scores of tapes and CDs, books and papers and pillows), I couldn't imagine that it held the secret to ending my writer's block.

Nevertheless, I decided that clearing out the clutter was easier than sitting there not writing, so I set to work organizing the various items and tossing the things we didn't need anymore. Eventually, I cleared enough away that I could see our hardwood floor. That's when my jaw dropped. There in the corner, up through a small hole that had been drilled for a cord to go through, a shoot of ivy was growing. It was maybe eight or nine inches tall and had a couple of leaves. It had wound its way under our house and up through the hole; clearly, it had been growing there for a while, but because of the clutter, I hadn't seen it.

This started me on a serious process of cleaning house. I enlisted the help of a girlfriend who is a professional clutter clearer, and she shared with me a great little book called *Clear Your Clutter with Feng Shui,* by Karen Kingston. The author suggests that when we're considering whether to keep or toss an item, we ask ourselves three questions. If we can't answer

yes to at least one of these questions, it's best to get rid
of it:

1. Do I absolutely love it?
2. Does it lift my energy when I think about it or look at it?
3. Is it genuinely useful?

Those questions brought remarkable clarity into my life.
I went to the mantelpiece, picked up a vase I had received as
a wedding present from Aunt Mabel, and realized that it actually
sapped my energy, that I never had (and never would) use it as
a vase and that, in fact, I hated it.

As I continued this clutter clearing throughout my house,
I got in touch with some resistance: *What if I need it some day?*
What if Aunt Mabel's feelings are hurt? What if I won't have
enough—vases, money, love? I recognized that many of these
thoughts are rooted in fear and that if I don't shift my thinking,
I'll end up re-creating the clutter.

As I was cleaning out the house, I passed by my calendar
and my to-do list. I decided to ask the same three questions
about what I had scheduled for myself and my family. Dentist

appointment? I don't love it, but it's truly useful. Dance lesson for daughter? Actually, as I thought about it, she didn't enjoy the lessons, and it made us both crazy trying to get there on time. As I went through all the various activities, I realized that some things were time clutter and that we could create more spaciousness in our lives by tossing them out.

I also became aware that I carry a lot of clutter in my mind. I can exhaust myself with thoughts like, *What if I'm not a good enough mother? The house should stay clean. I should be more productive. Things should be easier. People must treat me fairly. I won't be able to handle this.* All of these beliefs floating around my head sap my energy and are not at all useful.

So that dream was one that actually came true. I started to write again, and as we cleared out all kinds of clutter, my family and I began to relax and feel a sense of spaciousness in our lives.

Clearing-Clutter Practice

Take Karen Kingston's three questions and apply them to different areas of your life. Notice if you experience any resistance to empty spaces—in your home or in your day.

- First, look at the things that clutter your home. Take it a room at a time. Ask yourself if things give you energy or drain it, if you love them, or if they're useful.

- Next, look at time clutter. What things did you do today that you didn't really enjoy? What were things you didn't need to do? What activities or people drained you? Where could you schedule empty spaces on your calendar and in your children's schedule? Does a sense of spaciousness give you energy?

- Look at mental clutter. How much time do you spend rethinking the past or anticipating the future? Do you make a lot of judgments about yourself or others? Do you hold grudges? Notice the effect of all the "shoulds" on you. Do these give or take your energy?

As you let go of things that no longer contribute to your life, celebrate the fact that you now have more time and energy and space for the things that do!

Compassion

The Dalai Lama teaches, "We learn affection from our mother, not a guru. The guru comes later. First we receive the lesson of compassion from our mother by example." From the earliest moments of life, we are hard-wired for connection.

As we practice Momfulness, we develop the capacity to hold our own lives with a compassionate and loving heart. We learn to move closer to—or even embrace—what is difficult rather than brace against or close off from painful feelings.

The meditations and practices in this chapter help us grow our hearts as we extend this compassion toward ourselves, our children, and all others. We discover in our daily lives the boundless and mothering love at the heart of the universe moving in us and through us.

May our hearts open wide with compassion for ourselves, our children, and our world.

Late-for-School Practice

Children will teach you about *yourself.* They'll teach you
that you are capable of deep compassion, and also that
you are definitely not the nice, calm, competent, clear-
thinking, highly evolved person you fancied yourself to
be before you became a mother.
—Harriet Lerner, *The Mother Dance*

You know those mornings—when you're running late, everything
is going wrong, the kids are not cooperating, and you begin to
lose it—when you end up either feeling like you're the worst
mother in the world or your children are the worst children in
the world?

My friend Amy and I were talking about those kinds of mornings at lunch the other day. I figured she must be an expert at knowing what to do; she is a physician and teaches mindfulness courses to parents at a local hospital. She also has the opportunity to practice mindfulness every day as the mother of two young children.

When I suggested she was an expert, she laughed. "I've had some very ungraceful moments with my kids!"

After we shared some battle stories, she said, "There is a practice that helps on those mornings when I find enough grace to actually do it. It's called 'Late-for-School Practice.'"

Take any given morning. You've reached that moment when you are well past your calm, serene self. For the fifteenth time you've asked the kids if they are ready, and now one is crying and saying that he can't find his teddy bear, and the other is insisting on tying her shoes herself.

In that moment, you realize you are late. First, take a slow, deep breath—for *you.*

Become aware of your thoughts, your feelings, and your physical sensations.

Recognize how cranky or stressed you are.

Now take another deep breath—for your children. Notice what is going on with them. Did they go to bed too late? Do they want to be independent but don't quite yet have the skills? Are they discouraged? Do they want attention? Are they too young to understand the whole concept of time and how much is required to get where you're going? When we are able to understand our children's behavior, we can respond more effectively.

Finally, take a breath for the "Now what?" Ask yourself, *What is needed in this moment?*

Then choose what you want to do next: find the bear, or tie the shoes, or give a clear instruction, or simply settle into the fact that you will be late. Recognize that whatever is going on, it's not worth losing your sanity over.

Three breaths. One for you. One for your child. One for the "Now what?"

Over and over again—maybe *every* morning—we get to discover that we are not the perfect mom. If we are ever tempted to believe that we are, our children will bring us back to reality as they teach us our limitations.

Remember: this life is not about perfection. It's about practice—the practice of recognizing the grace that's present in each moment. The grace is always there. We just need to create a little space, a little breathing room, to be aware of it and to let it open us and soften our hearts.

So every morning (or afternoon or evening!) we keep practicing—paying attention to what is happening inside of us and outside of us and opening to the movement of grace. We don't remember to do this in all moments—or even most moments—but as we practice, we discover that little by little it gets easier for us to respond to ourselves and to our children from a place of wisdom and compassion.

Late-for-School Practice

Now it's your turn. When you're running late or feeling stressed:

- First, take a slow, deep breath—for *you.*
- Become aware of your thoughts, your feelings, and your physical sensations.
- Pay attention to what's happening inside you. Are some of your buttons getting pushed? Are these old patterns?
- Now take another deep breath for your children.
- Notice what is going on with them. What is it like from their point of view?
- Then take a breath for the "Now what?" Ask yourself, *What is needed in this moment?*
- See if you can find grace in the chaos.
- Then choose what you want to do next.

Pier Pressure

There is something wonderfully bold and liberating
about saying yes to our entire imperfect and messy life.
—Tara Brach, *Radical Acceptance*

A funny thing happened on our way onto San Francisco Bay.
We had been invited to celebrate a friend's fiftieth birthday at
a champagne brunch aboard a large Bay Cruise yacht. We
anticipated a wonderful day: the air was clear, the wind whipped
up small waves, and we had full views of Alcatraz and the
Golden Gate.

We sipped orange juice and champagne, toasting our friend as the boat began to pull out from the dock. But two minutes later, our party was interrupted by a voice over the loudspeaker.

"Due to high winds, we will be returning to the dock. It does not appear we will be able to sail today. We will advise you shortly."

We looked at each other in disbelief and decided to go out on the deck to see for ourselves. The wind, while strong, did not seem unusually so. The bay was full of sailboats moving swiftly across the water, as well as a number of cruise ships. Then we looked down over the railing, and we saw the real reason for our abrupt return. The captain had accidentally steered the yacht into the pier on the way out. Three huge log pilings were lodged under the boat's front end; pretty much half of the pier was now traveling along with us.

When the boat arrived at what was left of the dock, the voice spoke again. "Due to high winds out on the bay, we will not be sailing for safety reasons. But please continue to enjoy your brunch."

Laughter rang out among the passengers at this obvious denial of reality. It was a comical sight to watch people taking pictures of the broken pier while the crew kept insisting the problem was high winds.

ॐ

Here's the thing. We *all* run into piers, and we often end up with the equivalent of thirty-foot pilings hanging off our bows: our fears, our anger, our shame, our jealousy, our guilt, our inability to stay on a diet—all the things we'd rather not admit to or have anybody else see, all the ways we think we're inadequate or flawed. We tell ourselves there's something wrong with us when we feel angry or needy or confused or scared, and we keep rating ourselves, thinking we're only acceptable if we conform to some impossible standard. Mothers are pros at this.

But the fact is that none of us is perfect—as a person, as an employee, as a wife, as a mother. We are human. Period. We're a whole jumbled mix of positive and negative qualities. As psychologist Albert Ellis teaches, "We are fallible human beings." Welcome to the club. Our worth doesn't come from what we do but simply from the fact that we are alive.

So here's the challenge: to remember to become friends with ourselves in an unconditional way. When I'm obsessing over

something (*Why did I say that? I should've known better!*), if
I can catch myself and shift the way I'm talking to myself so
that I sound like a real friend (*Hon, you did OK. Just relax. You'll
be able to handle this.*), I feel so much better. I relax; I soften.

When we notice our thirty-foot pilings—anger, impatience,
jealousy, laziness—we can stop being ashamed about them or
denying them or covering them over with something else, and just
say, *Yep. There they are.* Without trying to fix them or make them
go away, we just become curious about them: What's this fear
about? Have I felt it before? How about this anger? We keep
noticing our patterns and habits in a friendly, nonjudgmental way.
It doesn't mean we have to like everything in ourselves; we just
learn to talk to ourselves with tenderness and humor. *Sweetie,
you know what this is about. Take a deep breath.*

By practicing unconditional friendliness, we also stop all this
rating of ourselves: *I'm a bad mommy. I'm overweight. I'm boring.
I'm a lousy wife. I could've done better.* Being such a harsh judge
does not help us improve; it makes us ashamed and fearful. If
we realize how a child would respond to such criticism, we might
begin to consider that famous "inner child" of ours and begin to
be kinder to ourselves. An added benefit of this practice is that as

we soften and welcome all parts of ourselves, we also open to accept our loved ones in a more compassionate way.

Lovingkindness Meditation

This is a twenty-six-hundred-year-old meditation. There are no set phrases; you can choose words and images from your own tradition so that they express what you most want for yourself, for your loved ones, and for all in this world. The one that follows is the meditation from Jack Kornfield's book, *A Path with Heart*:

May I be filled with lovingkindness.
May I be well.
May I be peaceful and at ease.
May I be happy.

Take a few deep breaths. Gently repeat these phrases. You may wish to imagine yourself as a young child or as you are now. Let feelings of love and care fill your body, mind, and heart.

- You can practice any time of the day—while you're carpooling, while cooking in the kitchen, while sitting at your desk.
- Write the meditation on a small card and put it where it can be a reminder to send yourself love.

~~ Expand the practice and direct the phrases to others.
Call to mind your child or a loved one. As you do, say the
phrases for that person:

May she be filled with lovingkindness.
May she be well.
May she be peaceful and at ease.
May she be happy.

You can do this for your spouse during the day. You might
also pray for friends, particularly ones who might be having a
difficult time:

May they be filled with lovingkindness.
May they be well.
May they be peaceful and at ease.
May they be happy.

Continue in this way, offering kindness and love to people
in your life. Include people such as the bank teller or the checkout
person at the grocery store. Open your heart to include all people
everywhere. Extend love and care to all animals, all beings, the earth.

May all be happy and well.

Walking the Night Hallways

We, like the Mother of the World, become the
compassionate presence that can hold, with
tenderness, the rising and passing waves of suffering.
—Tara Brach, *Radical Acceptance*

It is the middle of the night. My young child cries out, asking
for Mom or Dad to come.

I am beyond tired. Every part of me wants to stay under the
covers. *Please go back to sleep.* But the cries continue. With a
heavy sigh, I get up, stagger out into the hallway, go to my child.
I struggle with exhaustion and with my own need for sleep.

It helps me in times like these to realize that I'm not alone.
I imagine all the other mothers or fathers who are up at this same

hour, holding their children or caring for a sick family member. Wherever they are throughout the world, I feel a connection with those who are awake and responding to the call of love.

Some of these parents may be feeling more tired or more afraid than I am, so I can help by sending them love and strength. On another night, perhaps they will be sending this kind of support to me.

The following prayer has been a reminder to me of the honor of caring for those we love in this great circle of life:

Prayer of Caregiving
May the burden of caring
not feel so heavy
as I remember all who have
gone before me
and all who will come after me.
May I know myself to be part of a great dance
that circles and comes round again.
I give thanks for the privilege of caring.
I am home. I am home.
—Jane Ellen Mauldin, *Glory, Hallelujah!*
   Now Please Pick Up Your Socks

We can practice this kind of meditation during other moments of suffering throughout our day. When we are feeling alone or tired or overwhelmed, instead of fighting what is happening, we can just be with it. We can be like a mother to ourselves. We take a breath and say to ourselves, *I know you suffer. I'm here for you.* We can also send our love to others who suffer in this way.

By leaning into the difficult places rather than resisting them, and by holding the places of suffering, we discover our hearts softening and growing wider with compassion.

"I Am Here for You" Practice

When you feel tired or lonely or in some way unhappy, try this experiment. Instead of turning on the television or eating or distracting yourself, simply take a breath, put your hand over your heart, and say to yourself, "I know that you suffer. I am here for you."

- Some people find it helpful to imagine hearing these words from a loving God or sacred presence.
- Find the mother inside yourself that holds you with compassion.
- You can practice this when your family members are suffering.
- You can hold them in prayer or in your arms, and you can communicate, "I know that you suffer. I am here for you."
- You can do this with others who are suffering in a way similar to yours.

When Someone Deeply Listens to You

> When we are listened to, it creates us,
> makes us unfold and expand.
> —Brenda Ueland, *If You Want to Write*

Julianna looks out the window. "Ben is here!" she shouts. She races out front, runs across the street in her socks, and before he can get all the way out of his car she throws her arms around his neck. She hops up and down on tiptoe. Through the window, I watch my oldest and my youngest loving each other, laughing, hugging, bouncing. They hold hands as she leads the way back to the house.

Ben has stopped by to watch the documentary, *March of the Penguins,* with her. They have a running joke that his name is "Penguidle," and they've made a pact that they won't watch the movie for the first time with anybody but each other.

They go into the family room and turn on the movie. I hear them from the other room, and soon I am closing my eyes, just listening to their laughter. I don't hear all the jokes and banter, but I do hear the laughter. Julianna's is pure; it rings out like bells; Ben's is deep and hearty. They are in love with each other. They absolutely delight in each other's company. Back and forth they joke, laugh, sit in silence. Without seeing them, I know that she is cuddling up next to him on the couch, as close as she can possibly get.

She pulls out the best in her brother. He laughs so freely, he is a child again with her. At eleven years old, she has no pretense, no mask. The two of them offer each other easy laughter, delight, pure joy. They love to talk with and listen to one another.

I'm reminded of a poem written by a friend of mine, the poet John Fox. In it, John expresses the healing effect that real listening can have.

When Someone Deeply Listens to You

When someone deeply listens to you
it is like holding out a dented cup
you've had since childhood
and watching it fill up with
cold, fresh water.
When it balances on top of the brim,
you are understood.
When it overflows and touches your skin,
you are loved.
When someone deeply listens to you
the room where you stay
starts a new life
and the place where you wrote
your first poem
begins to glow in your mind's eye.
It is as if gold has been discovered!
When someone deeply listens to you
your barefeet are on the earth
and a beloved land that seemed distant
is now at home within you.

—JOHN FOX

When we listen deeply—to our children, our partner, our friends, to strangers, even to ourselves—it is, as John said, as if gold has been discovered. We help release in each other more of who we really are.

Notice how you feel when you are deeply listened to and then pass on the gift.

Listening Practice

Author Brenda Ueland has some suggestions about listening:

> In order to listen, here are some suggestions: Try to learn tranquility, to live in the present a part of the time every day. Sometimes say to yourself: "Now. What is happening now? This friend is talking. I am quiet. There is endless time. I hear it, every word." Then suddenly you begin to hear not only what people are saying, but what they are trying to say, and you sense the whole truth about them. And you sense existence, not piece-meal, not this object and that, but as a translucent whole. [*Strength to Your Sword Arm*]

- Today, listen underneath your child's words.
- As your child is talking, stop your internal dialogue with yourself.
- Listen.
- This is not the kind of listening that is passive, that says, "Uh-uh. Uh-uh," in a half-present way.
- This is not the kind of listening that chimes in with advice or opinions.
- Stop yourself if you notice yourself wanting to offer these.

This kind of listening communicates to the other person that he or she is loved and interesting and worthwhile—that you want to hear more.

This kind of listening can work magic.

No Good Very Bad Day

Parenting is a mirror in which we get to see the best of ourselves, and the worst; the richest moments of living, and the most frightening.
—Myla and Jon Kabat-Zinn, *Everyday Blessings*

J don't want to write about the difficult parts. It all starts feeling too boring to talk about how we should've known better than to head off to a crowded mall on a Saturday afternoon when we were all tired and hungry and cranky.

In the first three minutes, Julianna disappeared. After a short search, we found her scrunched in an alcove, hiding from us. I gritted my teeth at Paul and told him he needed to become decisive and to pick out his own clothes. Then I took Julianna by the arm and went outside into the cigarette-littered courtyard.

"Sit on those dirty cigarette butts until you decide to cooperate!" I said sternly. Out of the corner of my eye, I glimpsed people looking at us, and I hoped no one recognized me as the woman who gives talks on parenting. My hair was a mess and my blouse was dirty and I wanted to crawl out of my skin. My eyes were tearing up, and I heard myself telling my child things I normally would never say. I started wondering why anyone becomes a parent and why anyone goes shopping, and I lost all compassion for myself and others.

And I'm so sorry.

In that moment, I couldn't find the space within me to breathe. I was hurting and wanted to hurt back. I kept thinking my kids are spoiled and it is all my fault and Paul is a jerk and he and I are both lousy parents and everything is out of control.

Paul suggested we go home, and I faced the wall inside, the screaming place of *there's no good choice.* All the other people looked like they were having a swell time, and I didn't know why we couldn't.

We walked in silence. After a few minutes, I began to find the space inside to breathe. Julianna took my hand. I found myself softening and sensing a way opening back to forgiveness of myself and my family.

There are days when I feel like the worst mother in the world—days when I lose it, hardly recognizing myself as the nice person I once thought I was. It amazes me how quickly our buttons can get pushed, and negative energy can surge through us. Most of the time, this happens when our own childhood wounds get reopened or when old patterns emerge that have nothing to do with what's actually happening with our children in the present moment. If we can create some space to understand what we're feeling, we can ask ourselves what we need. It's likely that we're also feeling depleted in that moment—of sleep, food, energy, patience. Ask and listen: What do I need? What does my child need?

None of us is alone in experiencing this. We all have these moments when we explode, when we say or do things that we wish we never had. I'm not excusing them. But it's in these moments that we can learn forgiveness and compassion toward ourselves and those we love. This is our practice, and it's an incredibly challenging and profound one. It's only when we're willing to transform ourselves, bit by bit, that our world is transformed.

We can take our confusion, our anger, our impatience, and the negative seeds within us, which are also at the root of the world's problems, and acknowledge them, sit with them, hold them, work with them. We can develop a steadfastness within ourselves that enables us to not look away but rather to ask, as we look deeply, for the grace of transformation—the alchemist's miracle—so that these seeds become wisdom, and compassion, and generous action.

Those of us who have given birth learned how to breathe in a way that allows us to take pain and use it effectively to push new life into the world. We *know* how to do this. Even on days when we feel ourselves stretched to the point of tearing, we can breathe. On some days maybe that's all we can do; maybe that's enough.

When we hold our children, when we hold all that is going on in us and around us, we are engaged in a practice that is transformative, not only of ourselves but also of our family and of our world.

Forgiving Yourself Practice

First, on a sheet of paper, write down a memory of something you'd never want anyone to know about you as a mom—a time when you felt inadequate or ashamed. Is there a way you can understand this in light of your own childhood?

- Now take the paper and cut out words and phrases.
- Make a pile of all of them on the table.
- Mix them up. Rearrange them and make new sentences.
- When you're ready, pick up the whole pile and put it in a bowl.
- Then decide what you're going to do with the paper.
- You can fill the bowl with water in the sink or put it out in the rain.
- You can burn the paper, or you can throw it away, or bury it.

As you do this, recognize that you can forgive yourself. You can tell yourself the truth, saying what's unsayable, and you can still embrace all of who you are in a forgiving love.

You might want to say a prayer and imagine yourself held by a loving parent who loves you—just as you are.

Mobilize the Mothering Instinct

If we can mobilize the mothering instinct in all of us,
we could save the planet. It is inappropriate to be
dispassionate right now.
—Helen Caldicott (from a 1981 lecture attended by the author)

One summer day, three young children—Joanne, John, and
Andrew—were on a walk with their mother. A car was coming
down the street, when suddenly a gunshot rang out. The driver
of the car was mortally wounded; he slumped over the steering
wheel and swerved into the family. All three children died. Their
mother survived, although she never completely recovered,
physically or psychologically.

The year was 1976. The place was Belfast, in Northern Ireland. The driver was a member of the Irish Republican Army, and he was shot by a British Army patrol. None of this was new. This kind of violence had gone on for decades, killing many in its wake.

What *was* new was that a certain mother was there to be a witness. She heard the thud from her home as the car crashed into a fence, and she ran to the spot. As she took in the horror of the scene, a threshold within her was crossed. In that moment, her life changed. She was thirty-four, with two young children. Her heart ached, crying out, *Enough. The violence must stop.*

Without any conscious thought or planning, she began to run from door to door, yelling for people to rise up and put an end to the senseless violence. "It doesn't matter what religion or political party you belong to," she said. "It's time to act, to find another way." During the days and weeks that followed, she worked tirelessly to get people involved.

Radio and television reporters began to cover what she was doing, and she appealed on the airwaves to the Irish people to come together and march for peace. She had no background in peacemaking or activism, but she was driven to act. She circulated petitions, organized marches, tore down barbed-wire barricades, and initiated events between Catholics and Protestants.

The mother's name was Betty Williams. One woman who responded to her call was the aunt of the three children who had been killed—Mairead Corrigan. She and Betty began the Women's Peace Movement of Northern Ireland, which later became known as Peace People.

For their first rally, which was just days after the horrific incident, thousands of Protestant and Catholic women heeded the call. They took buses from their own neighborhoods and converged in Belfast. Though they had never met each other and though hostilities had previously divided them, they came off the buses and fell into each other's arms. Their shared grief at losing husbands, sons, and daughters united them. They decided to break free from their fears and anger and to act together on behalf of those they loved.

Within a month of the children's death on the street corner, tens of thousands of people were marching in Ireland and Britain, demanding change. The leaders of the main churches in Ireland issued a statement supporting the Women's Peace Movement.

In 1976, Betty Williams and Mairead Corrigan were awarded the Nobel Peace Prize. Betty says that she wasn't the one who started the peace movement in Ireland; she says it was the death of the three children that started it. She was merely the voice yelling out for them—putting words to something that many of the women of Ireland were feeling at the time.

Betty now works diligently for peace, human rights, and the nonviolent struggle for justice, and her work has especially focused on the plight of children around the globe. I had the privilege of meeting her several years ago. She was presenting at a conference, and her words to our group were powerful:

> I believe that women as the givers of life have done a good job of bringing children into the world. But we haven't done as good a job protecting that same life. I think the mothers of the world have got to come together in one united voice and show the world a different way.

I spoke with Betty afterwards in the hotel lobby, and she told me that everyone, whether they have kids of their own or not, needs to take a fierce and protective mothering stance and protect all children. She gave me a hug and told me that we must all keep doing the work. "The children need us," she said.

Mobilizing Your Mama Bear Instinct

We each need to find our own threshold: the point at which
we break free of our fear and act on behalf of those we love.
—Derrick Jensen, *Hope* Magazine

What is your threshold?
What do you care about?
What do you love?
Is there some action that's required to help those you love?

- Be passionate. Let the fierce and protective mama bear part of you give you the energy for any action you take.
- Invite others to work with you. Form a community of like-minded people.
- Join one of the many groups of mothers working on creative solutions.

Embodiment

Love is a bodily process. We literally shape each other through our touch and through the way we attend to and care for one another. Most of our communication is nonverbal, expressed through our bodies and not our words.

As mothers, we have been physically stretched in so many ways. Our bellies and breasts often have the marks to prove it, and our tired bones at the end of each day attest to the effort required to care for ourselves and our families. Attention to bodies takes time. We are not machines; we need physical closeness; we need to dance and sing and play and live close to nature if we and our children are to thrive.

As we practice Momfulness, we learn to value and trust our bodies, and we discover that using our senses is a wonderful way to become more mindful. This section has meditations and practices that focus on using our bodies to return to the present moment, on nourishing ourselves with beauty, and on communicating our full presence to our families through loving touch.

May we live fully in our bodies as we bless our families each day.

Hugging Meditation

When you hold a child in your arms, or hug your mother, or your husband, or your friend, if you breathe in and out three times, your happiness will be multiplied at least tenfold.
—Thich Nhat Hanh, *The Heart of Understanding*

*O*ne of my family's favorite meditations is the Hugging Meditation. We do this almost every evening, after returning home at the end of our busy days. It's easy to do; the way it differs from a regular old run-of-the-mill kind of hug is that when you give another person a hug, instead of letting go after a quick pat on the back, you hold the hug for *three breaths.* That's all there is to it!

When you're first learning to do this, you may laugh or feel awkward. That's OK. Take the first breath while you hold your loved one. In, out. On the second breath, keep hugging. Just notice what happens. Are your breaths getting in sync? How does your body feel? Be together, breathing your third breath.

Hugging is such a simple act. Yet when we feel held and touched and seen in ways that are far too rare in our busy lives, we realize that our bodies—and our spirits—are starving for that kind of touch. We long to simply be held, to have arms wrapped around us in a way that requires nothing of us but presence. Especially for those of us who are mothers, it provides us an essential kind of nurturing.

The Hugging Meditation works wonders at the end of the day as family members return home. During that transition time, my husband and I are often tired or a bit cranky. But if we take a moment to hug and breathe deeply three times, then we both truly come home.

You might also discover that children (and dogs) know that something wonderful is going on when they see this type of hug happening, and they want to be part of it. More often than not, the hug for two at our house is transformed into a group hug.

The kids actually abandon television or computers and come in to join us, and our little dachshund starts bopping her nose on our legs for us to pick her up.

Try doing a Hug Meditation with your spouse, with your children, with your friends. First breath. Second breath. Third. It is an experience of coming home.

Hugging Meditation

Invite your partner or child or friend to try a new kind of hug. (You might see
some eye rolling, but stay with it!) You can explain that it's not a back-slapping
kind of hug but one that will be simply the two of you holding the hug for three
deep breaths.

- In, out. In, out. In, out.
- Sometimes people find themselves laughing during the hug; sometimes
  it's hard to relax into it. It's all OK. It might take a week or more before
  you get comfortable doing this.
- A great time to practice a Hugging Meditation is when family members
  come in from work or school; another good one is at bedtime.
- Just breathe, hug, and come home to yourself, to the one you're hugging,
  and to this moment.

Body Blessings

When people are blessed they discover that their lives
matter, that there is something in them worthy of blessing.
—Rachel Naomi Remen, *My Grandfather's Blessings*

Our bodies love our children's bodies in so many ways. In family
life, bodies must be rocked, fed, held, washed, touched.

I'd like to add one more thing: blessed.

When our bodies are blessed, we recognize that they are
sacred, and we are healed in body and soul. As mothers, we
have the great gift of blessing our families each day in a multitude
of ways.

Water Blessing

When we wash our babies, we delight in their slippery, shiny, tender bodies. As they splash and discover the joy of water, it's easy to understand why water is seen universally as a symbol of blessing.

When we give our babies their baths and gently pour water over their heads, we can say a prayer, giving thanks for them, and asking that they be healthy in body and soul. We can also wash ourselves with the same pleasurable attention we pay to our children. When we take our daily shower or bath, we can receive the water flowing over us as a blessing, letting it cleanse and soothe us. It's a wonderful way to start our day. Blessing rituals that are built into our normal daily activities like this are much easier to remember to do.

Ponytail Practice

Brushing our children's hair can be a painful experience, not only for our kids but for us as well. We are often in a hurry when we do it and not as gentle as we could be. When we use this daily routine as a blessing ritual, we infuse what we do with mindful presence.

We softly touch our children's heads as we begin. We say a silent prayer of gratitude for these souls who are in our care. As we brush their hair, we bring to mind our children's beauty and strength. We ask for wisdom and guidance to mother these children in a way that allows their spirits to blossom. When we are done, we give our children a kiss and send them off with our love.

Laying On of Hands

When we or our children or partners need healing—in body, mind, or emotions—the laying on of hands is a powerful way to transmit love. We can bring our full presence to our touch and bless each other's bodies. Through our hands, we send not only comfort but real healing. As we touch our loved ones, we stimulate the production of endorphins, which are natural pain suppressors. Our touch also boosts our immune functions and makes our bodies more resistant to disease. So when we kiss our children's scratched knees or boo-boos, we quite literally help in their healing.

As mothers, it's a gift not only to us but to our families when we're willing to ask them to lay hands on us, to sit with us, to bless us with their healing love.

Gratitude Practice

As mothers, it's likely that our bodies are chronically exhausted. We can give ourselves a blessing, and we can express gratitude to our bodies for all they do. We might use words such as these: *Thank you for taking such good care of me and so many other people. I know you need _____ . I will do my best to take care of you. My prayer for you today is _____ .*

As a more extended body meditation, we can become aware of various parts of our bodies and express gratitude for their hard work:

Feet, thanks for all the places you've carried me today.
Arms, thank you for picking up and holding the kids so many times.

Head, thanks for all your thinking, daydreaming, and keeping track
of so many things.

During pregnancy, this is a wonderful meditation to do as we
thank our bodies for knowing just what to do to bring a new being
into life.

Coming-of-Age Blessing

There are many rituals or blessing ceremonies to do with family or
friends to honor transitions that involve our bodies: birth, puberty,
menopause, sickness and healing, death. We can incorporate our
own religious traditions into these blessing rituals, honoring our
bodies as sacred vessels at all stages of life.

Honoring-Your-Hands Practice

"Through the work of our hands, we bless our children's bodies."

- Spend a moment appreciating all the things your hands do with your family: prepare meals, do creative work, wipe foreheads of sick children, clean sticky fingers, change dirty diapers, pay bills, bathe slippery bodies, fold laundry.
- Recognize how love passes through your hands each day.
- Be grateful that your hands are the hands of a mother, administering the sacrament of ordinary life.

Seven Nights in a Row

One regret that I am determined not to have
when I am lying upon my
death bed
is that we did not kiss
enough.

—Hafiz (in *Love Poems from God,* Daniel Ladinsky, trans.)

A few years back, I was minding my own business, standing in the checkout line at the grocery store and reading the topics from women's magazines. It seems everyone needs to lose the same ten pounds, and it's comforting to know we can do it in one day if we buy a magazine.

All the magazines had the same themes: "Lose Weight," "Redecorate," "Have More Sex," and "Fattening Holiday Recipes" (so you'll be sure and buy the "Post-Holiday Weight-Loss" issue).

It was the "Have More Sex" headline I was curious about. This one was subtitled "Seven Days in a Row."

"You've got to be kidding," I said out loud—and then looked around to make sure no one heard me. I picked the magazine up and nonchalantly tossed it into my cart.

It had been a tough month for my husband and me, intimacy-wise. Our daughter was in preschool, and she had been coming into our bed every night at 4:02 A.M. Our three sons were full-blown teens, and they stayed up long past our bedtime, cooking mac and cheese and burning popcorn in the microwave.

Each night at dinner, Paul and I would catch each other's eye and wink. Maybe, just maybe, that night would be the night. But by the time we rolled into bed, all that happened was a yawn, a sigh, and telling each other, "Maybe in the morning."

So the magazine article intrigued me. As soon as I got home, I put in a video for my daughter and opened to the article. It even included pictures of a couple in bed on each day of the week: Sunday. Monday. Tuesday. Every single day. When I was through reading, I called Paul at work.

"Hi, Babe. I have a surprise for you when you get home," I told him. I gave him a few hints about what I had been reading. He left work immediately.

So, fast forward. The concept was great. Here's the reality:

First Night: We start out strong. We're delighted even to be *talking* about sex. After cooking, cleaning, checking home-work, hearing bedtime prayers, and giving kisses, we go running upstairs to bed, magazine in hand. We feel like teenagers and laugh as we get under the covers. Seven nights of this. This is going to be great.

Second Night: We don't run up the stairs quite as quickly, but we're still looking forward to getting into bed. We're a little tired but committed to this. The dog starts barking, and we have to interrupt to yell down to the boys to let him in.

Third Night: Three nights in a row! We're approaching territory we haven't been to in a few years, since before our daughter was born. We need to delay a bit until we fold all the laundry that is piled on the bed. After getting under the covers, we fall asleep while talking about who's going to drive the boys to school the next day. But we wake up really early the next morning and make up for lost time. We decide that this morning will count for what we missed last night, and that even though that's cheating a little bit, we're still on track for seven days in a row.

Fourth Night: We get into bed. It has been a long day. We take one look at each other, and I hear myself thinking the same line I said at the checkout stand: *You've got to be kidding!* But what I say is, "Well, sweetie, what are you thinking?" My husband, normally one who is up for anything that involves skin contact, looks like a football player who has had everything kicked out of him. But even so, he's still willing to go back on the field for the sake of the team. "I'm ready," he yawns. I snuggle up to him.

"How about if we just close our eyes for a couple of minutes?" I suggest. His answer is a snore.

Fifth Night: "Is this the fourth night or the fifth?" we wonder. We're falling behind. We look at each other, we look at our pillows. Not even a choice.

Sixth Night: What magazine article?

Seventh Night: We kiss goodnight. "Maybe early in the morning," we whisper.

Now that I think about it, I'm not sure there's a documented case of any couple with children successfully having sex seven nights in a row. I could be wrong. At any rate, we're still trying. "It's a worthy goal," my husband keeps reminding me.

Loving Touch

This is a great exercise for couples.

- Take some time with your partner to experience loving touch.
- Have your partner lie down and close his or her eyes.
- Gently touch your partner's face, neck, chest, arms, belly, legs.
- For this practice avoid the genital area.
  You want to focus on your sensations of touch.
- Alternate using your fingertips, your palms, the back of your hands.
  This isn't a massage; you are focusing on the pleasure of touch.
- Feel how it is to use short strokes, long strokes.
- Enjoy the experience without a lot of conversation.
- When you've finished, trade places.

Generations of Bodies

> It's also helpful to realize that this body that we have, this very
> body that's sitting here right now in this room, this very body
> that perhaps aches, and this mind that we have at this very
> moment, are exactly what we need to be fully human, fully
> awake, and fully alive.
> —Pema Chödrön, *The Wisdom of No Escape*

I come from a long line of women who didn't like their bodies.
In most of the pictures taken of my grandmother, she's posing with
her hand completely covering her face. I have to peer between
her fingers and try to piece together from memory what my Nana
looked like. This was a woman who did not want to be seen.

Her daughter—my mother—was also a product of an Irish Catholic upbringing. She didn't think one's body, especially one's breasts, should be visible. Her mantra to her daughters was, "Hide your headlights!" I was only allowed to wear baggy clothes all through high school—ironic, given that my bra size was AA. For years, I felt bad about even *having* a body and often wished that I was invisible.

Over the years I have struggled, as many women do, with body image. Actually, the experience of being a mother—of pregnancy, as well as nursing, bathing, tending, touching, holding bodies—has shown me how sacred and powerful my body is. I have been in awe of what it knows what to do.

Having a daughter has also helped. Julianna is turning eleven years old, and I love her body. I also love how *she* loves her body. She admires herself in the mirror and is delighted by how she's changing. The other day, she said, "Mama, when you look at me, what do you see?"

I answered, "A beautiful girl."

"Yeah, but what else?" she asked.

"A gorgeous girl?" I ventured.

"No, that's the same thing as beautiful."

Then, at virtually the same time, we both said the answer she had in mind as she looked at her own budding breasts: "A girl who is growing up so fast."

Julianna is on the threshold between innocence and adolescence, as comfortable running and climbing trees as she is wearing nail polish and fancy dresses. While I can't imagine telling her to hide herself in the way that my grandmother and mother told me to do, I am realizing that much more than just my words will affect her. She will absorb my own way of being comfortable inside my skin as a model of womanhood.

ॐ

Yesterday, my mother broke her knee while babysitting Julianna. My mother is in her seventies now, and she has severe osteoporosis. "Like Swiss cheese" is how her doctor described her bones; they are becoming white lace as her skeleton slowly softens, crumbles, finds its way back to earth.

My mother has broken both her wrists, her pelvis, her shoulder, and many ribs. Now it's her knee. She went up the stairs after all my warnings not to, and Julianna heard her topple down several of them and onto the flat floor. She ran to her grandmother, feeling guilty that she had been watching television and was not there to help.

As I sit now in the hospital, I hear tears, cell phones, and laughter as families in other rooms gather around the ailing bodies of their loved ones. My mother is anxious, and a nurse comes in and takes her hand; she applies lotion and slowly massages it while reassuring her that she'll be OK.

My sisters and I take turns sitting by our mother's side. I feed her blueberry yogurt, and my mouth opens spontaneously, as if urging hers to open. I fed my babies this way, in spoonfuls, tucking soft food between lips. Through tears my mother tells me, "This is just like I did with Nana." I know it is also the way she fed me.

Julianna comes with me, and I silently think, "Watch and learn, honey. This is how you feed a mother. One day, you may feed me." The three of us—three generations of women's bodies—sit together in the hospital room. We are family; we care for and tend to each other's bodies.

Generations of Your Body

Find pictures of yourself as a girl—as a toddler, as a ten-year-old, as a teen.

- Take some time with each and really *see* the girl in the picture.
- You might want to journal, asking your younger self questions and having her respond.

  What does she want to know about her body?

  What might you tell her if she was looking in the mirror and asked you what you saw?
- Write a letter from yourself at age eighty:

  "Dear Me,

  This is what I'd like to tell you about your body. . . ."

  Pay attention to what you tell yourself.

Saved by Wonder

If God said,
"Rumi, pay homage to everything
that has helped you
enter my arms,"
there would not be one experience of my life,
not one thought, not one feeling,
not any act, I
would not
bow
to.

—Rumi (in *Love Poems from God*,
   Daniel Ladinsky, trans.)

We pray not only with our hearts and minds and spirits; we pray with our bodies. We bring our hands together. We kneel. We bow deeply. We do full prostrations. We raise our arms in praise or supplication. Our spiritual traditions may vary in the prayer postures used, but each tradition knows the value of involving the body in experiencing the sacred.

A friend of mine, Carolyn Foster, told me a story of how one prayer posture actually saved a man's life. A number of years ago, UNICEF hired Carolyn to write a manual on healthy parenting practices. Her year of research and writing was interspersed with visits to Bangladesh, where the manual was to be field-tested. In that low-lying country, torrential flooding regularly killed thousands, and she heard many, many stories of heroism and good and ill fortune, told humbly, with Allah as the central character. One day, the man who was Carolyn's driver shared how prayer had helped him to survive a flood a few years earlier.

Knowing a big storm was approaching, he left Dhaka and went home to his village. He drove his wife, mother, and children to a less perilous location and then headed back, hoping to rescue his cow. Suddenly, a wall of water slammed into his vehicle, throwing him into the river that was now submerging the road. The currents were pulling him under, and after a long struggle, his strength was ebbing.

The man knew he was dying. He gasped and surfaced one last time.

In that moment, his eyes saw an incredible display of colors in the sky. The gray and black storm clouds had parted, revealing what seemed like a never-ending sunset of pinks, blues, and golds. Moved by such beauty, he spontaneously raised his arms in the traditional gesture of awe and wonder with which he had greeted Allah five times a day all his life.

In what seemed surely to be the last moment of his life, his left arm, raised in praise, caught on a protruding tree root. His body jerked to a stop. Astonished at this miracle, he clung to the tree until the waters receded.

As he finished telling my friend Carolyn the story, he said with deep conviction, "My life was saved by wonder!"

Perhaps many lives are saved by simple gestures of wonder, awe, and praise.

Prayer Postures

Today, deepen your connection with the sacred by involving your body in prayer or meditation.

- Do a prayer posture with your children, and let them remind you how to use your body to express wonder and joyful praise.
- Try a posture that you never have used before, such as bowing, kneeling, or lying flat on the ground.
- Or simply bring your two hands together in a gesture of prayer, gathering up all of your life and all that you love in your hands.
- Build into your day the simple habit of bowing or folding your hands at a set time: as you get out of bed and greet the day, as you gather together to eat a meal, or as you arrive at your front door at the end of the day.

Close to Things

Come on, I say to the creek, surprise me; and it does,
with each new drop. Beauty is real. I would never deny it;
the appalling thing is that I forget it.
—Annie Dillard, *Pilgrim at Tinker Creek*

At the beginning of her Pulitzer Prize–winning book, Annie
Dillard writes: "I live by a creek, Tinker Creek, in a valley in
Virginia's Blue Ridge." I read her words and realize that I, too,
live by a creek: Saratoga Creek. Only it is in a valley that has
the first name of Silicon.

This valley—a huge expanse of land encircled by hills and
bay—used to be called the Valley of Heart's Delight. I imagine that

here, in another day and age, it was easier to live close to things. Sometimes it now seems there is more silicon than heart. Is it a lack of trees, orchards, waterways that keeps us from living close to creation and to ourselves? Or is it too much concrete, so many freeways, too much speed? Perhaps here, as in so many other places, it is living a life in front of screens—TV, computer, movie—that pulls us away from a sense of connection with the natural world.

In earlier ages, the wise ones lived close to things and touched the face of God in wild places. The psalmist wrote of the restoration of soul that only happens near still water and in green pastures. Moses led his people into the wilderness, shed his shoes, and received on a mountaintop two tablets of stone from the One Who Lives. Buddha sat under the bodhi tree and, as he touched the earth, became the Enlightened One. Jesus was driven into the wilderness by Spirit after he heard he was beloved; he was sent into wilderness to learn what he needed to know. There in the wild he heard the big and breathing life of God that held him and all those around him—a life so inclusive it left no one out. Mohammed prayed and meditated in a cave, welcoming the angel in a mountain of light.

And so I walk to Saratoga Creek to learn how to live close to things. I sit in open places, lie down under trees, move into a larger space than the one behind my eyes. I go with my questions more than my answers. What might this ordinary, unassuming waterway teach me about motherhood, about a way to live a life?

It's early June, and the grasses are still green, tall and wafting in the breeze. The creek bed has small pools of water, mere leftovers from winter and spring rains. When the waters rushed through, it knew it was a creek; now, with its dry bed of small stones, it could be mistaken as merely a ditch. Ducks find the places where there is water, and the males fight over a lone female. A crow yells at me to stay away from its nest. A red-tailed hawk keeps watch from across the banks; lizards scurry below blackberry bushes. Squirrels are everywhere, chattering and dropping half-eaten nuts.

Years ago, I discovered what I thought was another creek when I went on a field trip with my daughter's preschool. We went to a park eight miles from our home. I loved that creek; it had lots of clear and flowing water, a small bridge to stand on, dancing light and shade created by willow, alder, sycamore, and laurel trees. Sounds of woodpeckers and children and water surging over rocks filled the park. After that day, I often dropped my daughter off at preschool and returned to the park to walk and write and pray.

So I was stunned—astonished—to discover that the creek by her preschool was the very same creek that is only blocks away from my home. It winds its way for twenty-five miles through Silicon Valley's cities and suburbs, from its source that is at an altitude of three thousand feet to where it eventually flows into San Francisco Bay. I was also amazed to find out that it runs through most of the parks that I have taken my children to for twenty-five years—the Squirrel Park, the Curvy Slide Park, the Duck Park.

How can this be? I have raised my children beside this creek and didn't even know it. I have driven on top of it on overpasses every day for decades. Where have I been? How can this creek have been so invisible to me? As I discovered that each new section was part of the same creek, I shouted, *This too? This is the same creek?* It was like redoing my life in my mind, like when you realize someone you know has been there all along: *You were there, too? And there?* I have loved this creek in bits and pieces, not ever realizing it was all the same creek. Like grace, this waterway had wound its way—invisible—through my life.

Years ago, my sons went to summer camp beside the creek, sneaking down its banks to examine dead possums and to learn how to skip rocks. When my world was turning upside down and I was going through a divorce, I sat by the creek and watched my young boys on the nearby playground. I sent my prayer to the heavens that they would be OK through all the changes, that they would always be friends with one another, that they would always know the way home.

In the days following September 11, 2001, this was the creek on the edge of the field where my daughter's soccer practice was held. In that scary time it was wonderful to resume practices and regain some sense of normal. We watched little girls run across the green field, and we smiled, even as F-16s were flying over our heads.

My children's schools bordered this creek. Each year my daughter's elementary school takes field trips down into its dry and stony bed. This year I went with them. I discovered that anise has the flavor of black licorice, that one side of the creek gets more sun, while the other is verdant and green, and that the cottonwood trees are not doing well. I watched boys poke the web of an orb weaver spider as it stayed unmoving, despite the stick. We talked about the effects of pollution and picked up cans and bits of plastic.

As I researched information about this creek, I discovered that one woman had made it possible for the children to take field trips into this natural environment. She was known as "The Creek Lady." When the water district wanted to cement over the creek banks to prevent flooding, the Creek Lady stepped in to stop them. She wanted to protect the natural environment of the section of creek near the school so that the children could learn about life and death, about growth and decay, about how to live close to things. She wanted the children to return each year, from kindergarten through fifth grade, to come and see, to find out the names of plants, to notice how this place changed from year to year. If the children were not there to notice the changes, who would?

She organized the children in a protest, and it proved successful. The water district left the section of the creek near the school in its original natural habitat. It was a rare victory in this day and age, because the things that children learn in the creek are not on the standardized tests. The tests don't ask the question, *Do you live close to things*? Federal funding is not tied to a child understanding the difference between species of birds, or knowing the habitats of lizards, or recognizing the smell of anise. What will be the consequences of not teaching our children about stewardship, and community, and a connection to this place we call home?

And what of us? What price do we pay when we are too busy to live close to things? Could it be that we, as a society, aren't even living close to our children? We set up our society so that teachers and doctors don't have time or energy to live close to our kids, to listen and watch and know what they, as individuals, need. As class sizes get bigger and appointment times get shorter, we treat one another as if we were machines rather than part of a diverse and beautiful world. For convenience sake, we become like creeks turned into cement channels.

So I come to the creek to remember how to live close to things. I come to it as a touchstone; I come to it to live more fully in my body, in touch with the natural world. The creek appears in my dreams, and its stones and water and trees and creatures often ease me back to sleep.

I recognize that in the grand scheme of things, Saratoga Creek will never be considered a great creek. But I've discovered that when you know one place well, through your soles and in your soul, you begin to understand the deep connection of everything to everything else. And by learning to love this one place, I care more about many places—rain forests, coral reefs, the arctic wilderness, the garden out my back door.

As I walk this creek, as I watch its shape shift—now I'm a creek, with waterfalls and wildlife; now I'm a cement drain, dry as a bone; now I'm wild again, with berry bushes and elms—I hear an invitation to discover life anew, in all its disguises. Like grace it winds its way through my life, unseen, always there.

Coming-to-Your-Senses Meditation

One of the best ways to become more mindful is to shift out of your head and into your body. Let your senses help move you into the present moment.

- Spend an entire day focusing on one of your senses.
- Involve your kids. Spend time together outdoors if possible.
- Put up a sign that reminds you what the "Sense of the Day" is. For example, on Monday, put your attention on your sense of smell.
- Be mindful during that day of all the things you smell: your morning coffee, roses, your child's warmth, rain, dish soap, dirty diapers.
- On Tuesday, pay attention to your sense of touch. Notice how things feel: a breeze, your baby's cheek, an ice cube, grass on bare feet, your dog's ears, warm water.
- Spend the next day on sight, then one on sound, and one on taste.

  This can be a week when your family lives with senses wide open.

- During meals, pass around spices or other things that you can touch, smell, taste. Take turns closing your eyes and guessing what they are. As a family, enjoy coming to your senses!

The Sacred
in All Things

Motherhood shifts our ideas about holiness. We don't need to return to an earlier age of miracles; we simply need to see what is in our own lives through new eyes. We discover the sacred residing not only in cathedrals but also in carpool lanes. We witness the Divine peeking through moments of silliness as well as silence, and we sense love's presence in our bodies as well as in our spirits.

As we practice Momfulness, we celebrate the holy in the ordinary. We build in "sacred pauses," creating rituals and traditions that help wake us up to the extraordinary moments of love and grace that wind through our everyday lives.

The reflections and meditations in this chapter invite us to nurture family spirit and discover the sacred in all things. May we open to the great love and grace that holds us all.

Where Does the Wind Come From?

If we had a keen vision and feeling of all ordinary human life,
it would be like hearing the grass grow or the squirrel's
    heart beat,
and we should die of the roar which lies on the other side
    of silence.
As it is, the quickest of us walk about well-wadded with
    stupidity.
—George Eliot, *Middlemarch*

One day not long ago, a little girl and her mother were driving down the expressway. The little girl looked out the window while the mother sped along, thinking of all that she had to do that day.

She barely heard her daughter when she began speaking to her from the back seat.

"Mama, where does the wind come from?"

The mother changed the radio station to listen to the news while answering her daughter's question. "Uh, I think it's when a high-pressure zone bumps up against a low-pressure zone, and that makes wind."

The mother was pleased with her recollection from science class and hoped the information was accurate. Then she heard her little girl say in a soft voice, "Oh. I got it wrong."

Fortunately, the mother was awake enough to hear her say this. She turned off the radio and looked in the rear-view mirror.

"Why honey? Where do you think the wind comes from?" she asked.

The little girl looked out the window again as she thought for a moment. "Well," she said, in deep concentration, "I think it comes from when waves reach up and try to touch the moon, and then they fall back into the ocean, and that makes some wind.

"And then the moon shivers, and stars come out from behind the moon, and that makes some more wind," she added.

"And once the wind begins blowing the trees, they move their branches to keep the wind going."

They arrived at a stoplight, and the mother turned around to look in her daughter's eyes.

"Oh sweetie," she said. "You didn't get it wrong." The mother realized that she was the one who lacked understanding. Her daughter lives in a creative and sacred world, with the eyes to see and the ears to hear the holiness all around her. The mother's prayer was to live with an awareness of such grace.

Sacred World Practice

Take a silent walk with your child around your neighborhood or at a park.

- Find a place where you can sit and just listen together to the sounds of nature.
- Let your senses come alive.
  What do you see? Hear? Smell?
  Are you aware of the holiness around you and within you?
- Sometimes you might bring along sacred scripture or poetry; when we read these outdoors, we can experience new insights, and it can help close the gap in our minds between the sacred and the ordinary.

Lobster Tale

Sitting around the table telling stories is not just a way of
passing time. It is the way the wisdom gets passed along.
—Rachel Naomi Remen, *Kitchen Table Wisdom*

Sitting around the table, we tell the story again. Paul is from
Maine, and he makes a wonderful baked stuffed lobster. One
year he made this specialty for his best friend Steve's birthday.
Paul bought the live lobsters, prepared them, put them in the
oven, and served them to our guests. Part way through this
elegant dinner, I began to smell something burning. I mentioned
it to the others, and sure enough, they smelled it, too.

We all stood up and began to go around the house to find the source of the smell. We checked the furnace, we felt the walls to see if they were hot, we checked in the oven and stove. Nothing. We went upstairs; we looked in the laundry room, the garage, the backyard; still we could not determine the cause.

We decided to call the fire department, just in case. I dialed 911.

"Hello. This is *not* an emergency, but we're smelling something like burning rubber and we can't figure out where it's coming from. Is there a way you could just send someone by to check it out?"

The operator asked, "How many people are in the house?"

"Eight," I told her.

"Have them all gather in the front room."

"OK, but I don't think it's necessary," I said.

Five minutes later, we heard sirens—lots of them. Three fire trucks, including a hook and ladder, rolled up to the front of our house. The firefighters came to the front door and began traipsing through. The five men were quite large (and, my friend Patt and I agreed, quite attractive), in full yellow and black gear. As they came in, they'd take a sniff, and say, "Yep, smells like burning rubber."

We went back to sit at the table while they continued their search. One firefighter asked permission to go upstairs to check my teenage son's bedroom. When the nice man came back down, he said with a smile, "Well, there *could* be a fire in there, but ya'd never know it!"

After a twenty-minute search, no luck. By that time, the smell had started to dissipate, and the firefighters decided that our furnace was probably the source. "You should probably go ahead and replace it," they told us. So the next week we did. The new furnace cost $1,800.

Fast forward a year. Now it is our friend Barbara's seventy-fifth birthday, and Paul has offered to make—you guessed it—baked stuffed lobster. He prepares the lobsters, puts them in the oven, and we sit at the table while they cook. All of a sudden, I start to smell something. Burning rubber!

My eyes widen as I look at Paul. I'm overwhelmed with a sense of déjà vu, wondering if I'm in the movie *Groundhog Day*. I go to the oven, open the door—and you know the large rubber bands they place on live lobster claws to prevent them from opening? Well, Paul had forgotten to remove them that night. The source of the burning rubber smell was found.

Suddenly, the entire story of Steve's lobster dinner and the sirens and the firefighters raced through my head. And then I realized that the $1,800 we had spent on a new furnace had been completely unnecessary. Apparently, Paul had forgotten to remove the bands that time as well, but we hadn't smelled the burning rubber until long after the lobsters had left the oven.

Every time we eat lobster, we tell the story. Guests laugh, and our kids chime in with remembered details. In the grand scheme of things, this isn't a great story or a profound story. There are no major life lessons or morals that we're imparting in its telling. What this story is, however, is one of many stories that not only describe but help to create the life of our family: *Listen. This is how love happens in our home.*

Stories weave families together. Birth stories, silly stories, life-and-death stories, Uncle Joe stories, sacred stories. Over and over, we tell them. We pass them on from generation to generation. In good times, in hard times, *this* is how we were together. This is how we made it through. This is how we lived and laughed and loved.

Story Time

- Have each member of your family choose a picture from your photo albums or boxes that they really like, one that portrays a memory they'd like to share.
- Have a family storytelling night. Let each person tell their story, beginning with "Once upon a time. . . ."
- Encourage the embellishing of stories.
- Ask family members to chime in at the end of each story with their own version.
- Listen to how your family is woven together—and to how love happens in your home.

Framing the Day

I have a lovely habit:
at night in my prayers I touch everyone
I have seen that
day;
I shape my heart like theirs
and theirs like
mine.
—St. Teresa of Avila (in *Love Poems from God*,
    Daniel Ladinsky, trans.)

Many days we wake up and hit the ground running, and
we don't stop until we fall into bed exhausted, after the last

child has gone to sleep. If we live day after day this way, life begins to feel like a treadmill we can't step off of, and we remain unconscious of so many extraordinary moments of grace.

Several years ago, I heard a radio interview with a Tibetan monk who now lives in the United States. He spoke about how life in Tibet is completely organized around spirituality, from the moment one wakes up until the moment one goes to sleep. These built-in practices help people be more aware of the spiritual dimension of life. Here, however, he sees that things are very different. "It is very hard to live in a society that is organized around shopping," the monk said softly. He is a very wise monk.

As a way of cultivating our practice of Momfulness and of enhancing our ability to sense the sacred in our lives, we can bracket each day with a frame of intention and gratitude: We begin the day with a morning offering or setting of intention and end with an evening prayer or meditation of gratitude.

Morning Offering

When we first wake up in the morning, we are usually off and running in our minds before our bodies even get out of bed—things we have to do, conversations we're rehearsing, worries or anxieties we're feeling. It's all there before our eyelids even open.

Can you envision that brief moment between sleep and wakefulness? What if you just stayed in place for a moment or two? When you wake up tomorrow morning, let your plans wait another few minutes. Take a moment to notice the tiny opening into the new day before your busy mind takes over. Breathe in and out. Welcome the day. Be aware of your body. Settle into it. Smile. The door of this new day is opening.

Welcome the morning, perhaps with a prayer. You might offer the day to God; you might set an intention to be of service during this day; you might ask to be aware of the gifts of the day as they arrive.

After a while, you may look forward to this moment of offering and stillness. As a way of remembering this practice before you jump out of bed, you might want to place a symbol on your ceiling or your dresser to remind you to pause when you open your eyes to the new day.

You can also build the morning offering into your other morning routines: when you are making your coffee, taking your shower, sending your children off with kisses and blessings, or stepping outside to go to work. When we incorporate spiritual practices into everyday habits, it's much easier to remember to do them.

Evening Prayer

Bedtime—the transition from light to darkness—is a natural time for prayer. It is a time for rituals and storytelling and kisses and prayers—reminders to us that even in the great darkness, we will be held.

At the end of your day, perhaps when you're saying prayers with your children or when you're under the covers in your own bed, take a few minutes to be mindful of your day. Recall your morning prayer. The day has passed, and now you are here. Evening has come. Know that this day was held in love, even with all its stresses or challenges.

Think of one moment of delight when you laughed or smiled today. Name two or three things for which you are grateful. Where did you experience the Sacred today? Where were you surprised? When you pay attention to the good things of a day, no matter how seemingly small, you send your body the message that it can relax. Express your gratitude for all the gifts of the day.

Lighting a candle, listening to quiet music, writing in your journal, or going for an evening walk and looking up at the night sky are also wonderful ways to close the frame of your day and welcome the night.

Framing Your Day

Tomorrow, bracket your day with a frame of intention and gratitude.

- Begin the day with a morning offering or setting of intention, choosing a practice that you can do regularly.
- End your day with an evening prayer or meditation of gratitude.

Nurturing Family Spirit

Spirituality is the sacred center out of which all life comes,
including Mondays and Tuesdays and rainy Saturday
afternoons in all their mundane and glorious detail. . . .
The spiritual journey is the soul's life commingling with
ordinary life.

—Christina Baldwin, *Life's Companion*

The moment was a serious one. The large extended family was
gathered around the table for Thanksgiving dinner, and they were
getting ready to say grace. Everyone was supposed to say one
thing for which they were grateful, but when they went around the

circle and got to five-year-old Emily, she was embarrassed. She put her napkin over her head and sat in silence.

Nobody moved. They looked out of the corner of their eye at her mom and dad, to see how they might respond. Mom's face became stern, and as she was about to correct Emily, Grandma did something totally unexpected. She put her napkin over her head.

The family started chuckling. Then two cousins covered their heads with their napkins, and soon Aunt Jane and Grandpa joined in. Before long, the entire family was sitting around the Thanksgiving table with napkins over their heads.

That happened twenty-five years ago. At every Thanksgiving dinner since then, just before eating, the family gathers to say grace. Then they wait with smiles to see who will be the first to put the napkin on the head. This year, Grandma was no longer with them, and it was the first time that Emily's daughter was able to sit in a high chair near the table. Even though family members changed over the years, what has remained constant is the love and the laughter and this simple ritual that binds them all together as a family.

When we celebrate moments together, from family dinners to bedtime rituals to holiday celebrations, we strengthen our families. We create lasting memories, we give our children a sense of security, we share our spirituality with our children, and we deepen a sense of belonging.

In past generations, rituals were much more likely to happen automatically through one's community or religion. But in modern-day life, with families often separated from relatives or no longer connected with their childhood faith traditions, new rituals and traditions may need to be established. Mothers are often the primary ritual makers in families, and it's so important that we take the time to create these "sacred pauses" in our otherwise busy days.

So light a candle, sing a song, say grace before meals. Slow down and recognize the connection and the celebration, the mystery and the miracle, that are present in our everyday lives.

Sacred Pauses

Terry Tempest Williams states,

> Our needs as human beings are really very simple—to love and be loved,
> a sense of connection and compassion, a desire to be heard. Health.
> Family. Home. The dance, that sharing of breath, that merging with
> something larger than ourselves. [in Derrick Jensen's *Listening to the Land*]

Are there some rituals that can nurture your family's spirit? A good place to begin
is by thinking about traditions or rituals that were meaningful to you as a child.
How might you continue those rituals or adapt them to your family now?

- Ask your children or partner what their favorite traditions and rituals are.
- Build in at least one daily ritual of connection (a family meal, bedtime
  prayer, goodbye hugs) and a once-a-week one (family night, religious
  service, meal at grandparents' house).
- As a family, celebrate holidays, important milestones, and rites of passage.

Grace

I do not at all understand the mystery of grace—only that it meets us where we are but does not leave us where it found us.

—Anne Lamott, *Traveling Mercies*

And then there's grace.

Grace is there when you bring the baby home and you don't know how to change a diaper and you think you're not the real mom. No matter how inadequate you feel, grace is underneath, supporting you, holding you.

Grace is there when you haven't got a clue, when you feel like the worst mother in the world, and when being a mom is so much harder than you ever thought it would be. It applies the gentle push on your back that keeps you going.

Grace is sometimes your only companion in the middle of the night when you're teetering on the edge of sleep deprivation and exhaustion, and the baby needs more. It's what keeps you from going crazy when you are awake at one in the morning, waiting and worrying in every passing minute for your teenager to get home.

Grace comes in laughter; it hides and then pops out, right after you've yelled at your toddler and then he says something so funny you can't help but smile, and the knot inside relaxes, and you realize you'll get through this OK. It's there in forgiveness, of yourself and of your family.

Grace catches you when you grieve, when your child gets the diagnosis you feared or you suffer unimaginable loss. It's there in the darkness as you weep after the divorce, when your children are no longer with you every night to tuck in.

Grace is there, even when you're not mindful or compassionate, when you're not present or forgiving; it waits patiently for you to let go into it. Grace comes through the support of friends; it reassures you with their smiles, with their understanding nods of *Yes, I understand, I know it is so hard!*

Grace holds you up when you feel completely unappreciated because no one sees all the thousands of little things you do in a day. Grace sees.

Grace winds through your life invisibly, though you often can't see it until you look back and recognize it in your children's growing bodies, in their quick wit, their caring comments, their embracing hugs.

Grace reveals to you a great mothering love that you can step into, that's been here before you and will be here after you. Grace will be with you as you open your arms, as you release your children and send them out into the world. If you listen carefully, you can hear grace whispering its thanks to you for being a mother to these souls.

Recognizing Grace

The words *gratitude* and *grace* come from the same Latin word *gratus,* meaning "pleasing." When you are feeling grateful, you will often sense the presence of grace. Having a nightly gratitude practice is a wonderful way to glimpse the movement of grace in your otherwise busy life.

- As you lie in bed at night, reflect back on the day. What are you grateful for? Counting these things is a great way to fall asleep.
- You might also reflect on, "Things I didn't see today."

By becoming more conscious of what you missed, you're more likely to recognize grace as it moves through your life.

Family Circle

There came a moment in the middle of the song
when he suddenly felt every heartbeat in the room
& after that he never forgot
he was part of something much bigger.
—Brian Andreas, *Trusting Soul*

J knew this day was coming from the moment I gave birth, when my child moved outside my protective belly. Benjamin, my oldest son, was leaving home.

For eighteen years, I had held him, hugged him, yelled at him, worried about him, and loved him. Through it all, time just kept moving forward, bringing us to this day. He was leaving in a few weeks for college, and even though he'd be returning for vacations, things would never be quite the same.

This is what's supposed to happen, I know. But when it does, when it's right in front of you, there is a sadness in knowing that the relationship will be changed forever. It is the end of a chapter of parenting—a launching of a child into the world and farther away from you than ever before.

Because this felt like such a major transition, I wanted to find a ritual that we could do with our family and friends. I wanted to send Ben off with a blessing, and I knew this could help me, too, in my letting go.

Ben and I talked about what such a ritual might look like. I mentioned a Native American ritual called the Giveaway: when people are married or have babies or graduate, they don't *receive* gifts, they *give* gifts. They want to thank the people who have supported them, who have been important to them, and who have helped them reach their accomplishment. It's a ritual that acknowledges a person's dependence on community.

Ben liked the concept of this, and he set to work planning it. When the day for our gathering arrived, twenty-five of us squeezed into our living room. I put on a CD of Barbra Streisand's song *If I Could.* It's a song she dedicated to her son, and it captures a mother's wish to do all the things she would if she could: change the world, teach her child all the things she never learned, shield her child from pain. Ultimately, it is a song about a mother watching her child grow and then letting the child go.

During the song we watched a slideshow I had put together: Ben as a newborn being brought home in a hospital Christmas stocking. Ben with a bowl of spaghetti upside-down on his head. Ben holding his new baby brother, David, then two years later holding another baby brother, Matt. Ben swinging on monkey bars, kicking the soccer ball, showing off his diploma from elementary school, from junior high, from high school. All of these were less than a fraction of all the moments that made up our life together.

At that point, when all of us were teary-eyed, Ben said that he had something to give each of us. On slips of paper, he had written down a gift that he had received in his life from each person: Paul had gifted him with humor, Steve with enthusiasm, Barbara with inspiration. He went around the room and thanked each of us for the gift we had given him and told us how we had influenced his life. On the paper he gave me, he wrote, "Thank you, Mom, for seeing me for who I really am."

In a few weeks, Ben would leave home. But he knew that he would never really be out in the world totally on his own. He would always have this little community—people who loved and cared for him, who will always be home to him—no matter how far away he goes. Even Julianna, who was only three years old, understood this. As we ended our blessing ritual, she tugged on my sleeve, looked around the room with wide-eyed delight, and said in a loud whisper, "Mama, all my people are here!"

Giveaway Practice

Is there an opportunity coming up when you and your family might honor the people in your life who have supported you? A major birthday? A graduation? A baptism?

- Make a list of the people in your circle of support.
- On a regular basis, communicate gratitude to "your people."
- Let them know how much they mean to you.

Community

As mothers, we feel better when our children are happy and healthy. When we are frazzled and stressed, our families are negatively affected. Relationships are at the heart of everything. We are all connected.

The Shona people in Zimbabwe acknowledge this connection in the way they greet each other: "Good afternoon; how are you?" one person asks, and the other responds, "I am well if you are well." The first person then says, "I am well, so *we* are well."

This is also true on a larger level. We live in a profoundly interconnected world. This final chapter focuses on the power of community, whether in small circles of support, in communities of faith, in social policies that foster well-being, in the global community, or in the wider community of Creation. As we practice Momfulness, we recognize that our children don't live in a vacuum; their future is tied to the future of others and to that of the earth. Our mothering includes rolling up our sleeves and working for a world in which all children can thrive.

May we care for each other and for the earth, and draw wide the circle of our family.

Sacred Circles

I don't know what in the world I would do without [female friends] for advice, for comfort, for simply knowing that there is someone out there who knows me as I am, and loves me despite and because of it.

—Anna Quindlen ("Some of my best friends are women," *The Houston Chronicle,* March 2, 1997)

It is early November—the month of giving thanks, the time of year when, even here in California, the leaves turn red and gold. I drive in the morning drizzle across the Golden Gate Bridge to meet with a circle of new mothers. These women call themselves

"The Sacred Mamas," and they gather with their babies to support each other in this new place of heart-opening love.

As I enter the room, I see babies, breasts, and blankets. One mother yells "Ouch" as her nipple gets bitten by her baby girl, who is discovering a new tooth. Another is comforting her son, who just tipped over and bumped his head; his sitting ability is not quite developed. Two other women are exchanging recipes for homemade baby food.

The group has invited me to share with them some practices on how to be mindful in family life, on how to stay in touch with their own interests and passions, and (most important) on how to stay sane. "Is that all?" I ask. "How many months do we have?"

We begin with a few moments of meditation, which, with babies, is never silent. Then I ask them, "What has your baby taught you?" Their answers come quickly:

"I didn't know I could ever love someone so much."
"I'm realizing that it's not all about me anymore."
"I'm learning patience."
"Patience."
"Patience!"

We talk for almost an hour, and it brings back many memories of those early years. I sat in a women's circle like this one right after I was a new mom. It was such a raw and vulnerable time, and it made all the difference to receive the advice and comfort and laughter of other women. Looking back, I realize now that so many of the things I obsessed about back then were not really that critical in the grand scheme of things: how soon my baby sat up compared to other babies, what his first solid food would be, whether I sterilized the pacifier after it fell on the floor. We all go through these worries as new mothers, but too often we are left on our own without the benefit of a supportive community.

I've heard that some cultures honor a new mother by taking her into seclusion with her baby for a few weeks so that she can be cared for and so that she can learn how to mother. Other women tend to her body, talk with her, and teach her how to feed and nurture and cherish this new child of the community who is bringing a great gift for all. What a difference that kind of support can make!

In addition to small circles of support, it's so essential that we, as a society, find ways to support mothers and families. So many mothers today are stretched to the point of breaking, and the result is that everyone suffers. The health and well-being of our entire community will be enhanced when we do a better job honoring the role of raising children, when we give parents paid family leave, flexible work hours, a living wage, excellent and affordable child care, and health care for all children. Through doing these things, we create a sacred circle, collectively caring for the next generation.

As I leave the Sacred Mamas circle and drive home across the bridge, I notice that the sky has cleared. I look out over the bay beneath me, and I think of my children—three of them already grown—and realize how much I have changed through being their mother. I offer a prayer for all new mothers, and I'm filled with gratitude for the circle of life.

Sacred Circles

Do you belong to a circle of friends who can support you and celebrate with you? Is there a community that has spirituality as a central focus? If not, you might want to gather a few friends and begin one.

Many groups are actively involved in supporting mothers and their children and in working toward more family-friendly social policies. Get involved with one or more of these as a way of expanding the sacred circle of family.

Our Many Mothers

Growing up in a Village meant being the child of the community. I was almost six years old before I understood that I came out of one particular person's womb, and not all of the women in the Village who had helped to care for me.

—Sobonfu Some (www.Sobonfu.com)

We have many mothers—people who have come along and loved us into wholeness. Their acts of kindness, their willingness to see us, to be there for us, to support us in ways that perhaps our own mothers couldn't, are all ways that they have mothered us.

One of my mothers was a woman named Sandra. She never had kids of her own, but she was the archetypal Mother in her embrace, her presence, in the love that came through her eyes, in her humor, her steadiness of spirit, her courage in the face of difficulty and pain, and in her nurturing of others' dreams along with her own.

It wasn't until she was dying that I realized her role in my life. Her breast cancer had metastasized, and fluid was filling her lungs. When I went to visit her, her eyes lit up when she saw me. "Oh, Denise," she said sweetly, her arms reaching out to hug me. I loved how she said my name. It reminded me of a quote by a four-year-old boy: "When someone loves you, the way they say your name is different. You just know that your name is safe in their mouth." That's exactly how it felt.

In the midst of her pain, Sandra smiled as if we had all the time in the world. "How are you? Are you writing?" She always asked about my writing. I longed to have as much faith in myself as she had in me.

As I sat there, I remembered what author Anne Lamott's doctor told her when her best friend was dying: "Watch her carefully right now, because she's teaching you how to live."

Sandra pointed to the tall, grey oxygen tanks that lined the wall of her bedroom. "I call them my generals," she laughed. As she slowly made her way to the bathroom, her caretaker told me that she was barely eating and that she was on morphine to help stop the fibrillations of her heart. It was clear that she would not live much longer.

When Sandra returned, she motioned for me to come and sit with her. We spoke for some time, sharing laughter and some stories. She told me that she used to dress up like a clown and visit with children and other people who needed a smile. "My name was Calypso, and I wore a black hat with an orange daisy, and an orange wig and a red nose. I painted a small red heart in the middle of my forehead." I loved imagining Sandra as a clown.

After a while, she closed her eyes and asked if I would pray with her. I put my arms around her, and we sat there in silence. Then I began to sing, letting go of words, just letting the music come through me. Sandra's body, full of morphine and cancer and so much love, slowly relaxed.

She loved music, and she especially loved singing. It was at the heart of her spiritual practice. She treasured both Western and Eastern religious traditions: on Sundays she'd go to church, and on Fridays she'd gather with a spiritual community to chant sacred texts in Sanskrit, as well as the many names of God. The music held her like a mother, like the mother that she herself never had.

When I stopped singing, Sandra slowly opened her eyes and smiled. "That was lovely," she said. "I'd like that when I'm passing."

I knew I couldn't make that promise, but I trusted that on the next part of Sandra's journey, there would be music. All the music she had created in her life would accompany her into the next—the way she was a song to all those who met her, the way she sang our names, the way she invited us to sing our own songs.

A week later, Sandra died. For her memorial service, we printed several photos in the program, including the photograph of her dressed as Calypso, the clown. We sang our hearts out, and we called each other by name. I shared my reflections about her being one of my mothers, and I saw many heads nod in tearful recognition. That day, so many of us discovered that Sandra had been a mother to us all.

Your Many Mothers Reflection

In a journal, write down your reflections on the following questions:

Who has been a mother to you?

Who are the people who have seen you, who have supported you?

Who has nurtured something in you that might not otherwise have
    been developed?

Who has been a compassionate presence in your life?

Perhaps there is someone you'd like to express your gratitude to. Find
a way in the coming weeks to do so. You might also reflect on who you are a
mother to—not only your own children but other people you nurture in your life.

The Holy Family Commutes

It is in the shelter of each other that people live.
—Irish proverb

They're here! They're here!" shouts four-year-old Tommy. His mother opens the door as he jumps up and down. Standing on the porch is a family from our church community, and they are carrying three statues—one of Mary, one of Joseph, and one of a camel. The sculptures of flat hammered brass, about eighteen inches tall, are modern and elegant in their simplicity. "Do you have a place for these visitors to stay tonight?" asks the family at the door. "We do! We do!" Tommy says. "Come in!"

The family brings the statues inside and places them on the coffee table next to an Advent wreath. During the next hour, the two families share hot cocoa, ginger cookies, laughter, and an evening prayer. After warm goodbyes, Tommy closes the front door. He asks if he can show Mary, Joseph, and the camel to his toys; one by one, he carries the statues to his room. There he introduces them to his trains and stuffed animals and many dinosaurs. Before Tommy crawls into bed, he places the travelers carefully on his nightstand and has a long conversation with them in the darkness.

A scene very similar to this one will be repeated many times in our community during the weeks of Advent. It is our church's annual enactment of Las Posadas (meaning "lodging" or "shelter" in Spanish)—a traditional celebration from Mexico that commemorates the Holy Family's search for a place to stay in preparation for Jesus' birth.

In our adaptation of this ritual, people take statues of Mary, Joseph, and a camel from home to home for four weeks, with each individual or family hosting these guests overnight. Then that family, in turn, carries the travelers to another home.

As church members deliver and receive the figures, they have the opportunity to share music, food, conversation, and friendship with two other families. They also record their thoughts and prayers in a cloth-covered journal that accompanies the Holy Family from home to home. At the end of the month-long journey, Mary, Joseph, and the camel arrive at our church on Christmas Eve. They are placed in a larger nativity scene, and we weave their arrival into the beginning of our Christmas Eve service.

To a casual observer, the brass figures appear to be three simple statues. But sometimes the simplest things are the most sacred. As I sit and read the entries made in last year's journal, I recognize that these little statues carry not only a great story— a pregnant woman and her husband seeking a place of safety for the child's birth, a child who will bring light to a darkened world—but also the stories of our community. As Mary, Joseph, and the camel travel from home to home, they bring along with them the stories and energy and spirit of each household. They connect us with an invisible thread, and I realize that we are all on a journey together.

Last year, Margaret, who had been recently diagnosed with leukemia, made the first journal entry. She had just completed a painful and exhausting round of chemotherapy, and her immune system was compromised, so she couldn't have many visitors. Although only one couple brought the statues to her home, she felt blessed by the entire community. A few weeks later, Margaret died of pneumonia.

Another entry was from Louise, who had lost her forty-year-old son a few months before to a sudden illness. Her son's death challenged her faith to its core, and she bravely struggled and prayed for a sense of inner peace. She placed the statues carefully on her mantle and wrote, "Today I thought of Mary's tragedy losing a young son, and I gained comfort from her."

I smiled as I read other entries. Tim and Amy were expecting their first child. They described sitting by the fireplace and talking about how that year had been a preparation for the child to come. They realized that the thoughts they had about their own baby were probably not too different from the thoughts, hopes, and dreams that Mary and Joseph had as they walked the streets in search of lodging. Amy wrote, "We thought it appropriate to place Mary and Joseph in our soon-to-be-born baby's crib so they might feel at ease, knowing their baby will have a warm place to come into the world."

There are a number of entries from children, expressing their delight in hosting the Holy Family, especially the camel. One boy played the piano for the honored guests; another set out special

food for each one. Many included the statues in their bedtime
rituals, as they said prayers of gratitude and prayers for those
who have no shelter or warmth. Even the adults experienced
the sense of something sacred in their midst. One mother of two
young sons wrote about how real the statues seemed to her.
"The next morning I found myself thinking in the shower, I'll have
to be quiet when I go into the kitchen. I don't want to awaken
my guests. Strange how such inanimate figures took on a life of
their own!"

As I read the entry I had made, I was reminded how my
then four-year-old daughter, Julianna, welcomed our visitors.
She introduced the camel to her stuffed Rudolph the Red-Nosed
Reindeer, and the two animals became fast friends. At bedtime,
she set the statue of Mary on my nightstand and put Jofus (her
pronunciation of Joseph) on her dad's nightstand. The camel
spent the night next to Julianna's bed.

As each year passes, this archetypal journey begins again.
Children, as well as adults, excitedly open doors and make room
for the travelers. Light, music, prayers, food, and friendship come
into our homes, creating sacred space. This is a simple ritual,
and yet it carries with it a warm and lasting grace. It helps us feel

connected, not only to our community but also to something larger. We recognize, with a smile, that we are all part of a Holy Family as we make our way in the world, as we seek and give shelter, as we love one another, and as we bring life into our world.

Holy Family Practice

Do you belong to a church or synagogue or other community that has family rituals built into the year? If not, get together with one or two other families with children of similar ages as your own and create an annual ritual.

Holidays are a natural time for these celebrations. Focus on a sense of community rather than on material things.

Are All the Children In?

The problem with the world is that we draw the circle of our
family too small.

—Mother Teresa

Several years ago, I heard Reverend James Forbes, the pastor
of Riverside Church in New York City, recounting a boyhood story
of a ritual his family did each night around the dinner table. His
mother and father gathered with their eight children, and just
before they said their blessing over the meal, his mother asked
a simple question: "Are *all* the children in?"

If a child was not present, they stopped and prepared a plate for that child and put it in the oven. Only after this was done did they say grace, pray their Bible verses, and eat. Reverend Forbes went on to say that he thinks of God as Momma Eternal, who asks *us* each day, "Are all the children in?"

The question stayed with me ever since I heard Reverend Forbes tell this story. I found myself sharing it with groups, writing about it in my journal, talking about it with friends. I wasn't sure what to do with it, except to keep listening to it.

Then one day, I read a newspaper article. It began:

WANTED

Flexible, big-hearted and internationally minded families to help young refugees achieve self-sufficiency.
Reward: A chance to help a child build a new life.

The article went on to describe a program starting up through our local Catholic Charities, in conjunction with the United Nations, called the Unaccompanied Refugee Minors program. They needed foster families to care for teens who had been forced to leave their homes and countries due to war or persecution.

Most of the kids were orphans or were separated from relatives, and many had lived for years in refugee camps.

As I read, I started crying. I wasn't even sure why, but for a good hour I sobbed. Something in me opened, and all my feelings of grief about the state of the world, especially for our children, just spilled out. Reading about the stories of these young teens— from Iraq, Afghanistan, Iran, Somalia, Sudan, and so many other places—who needed a family here in the United States, reminded me of the question: *Are all the children in?* I knew that the answer to that was *no.*

After a while, my tears stopped, and I went back to my regular day. *There's no way we could take in a teen,* I told myself. *It would be too much work. My kids would never agree. It's a nice idea, but get realistic,* I heard myself say. *It would change everything.*

When Paul arrived home, I mentioned it casually. "Hey, I read this article today. Take a look." I showed it to him. "You know, I had this silly thought that we might attend the information night. But if you don't want to, that's fine."

To my great surprise, Paul wanted to go to the meeting. "Why don't we just go see what's required?" he told me. "We don't have to make any commitment yet."

So the next night we found ourselves in a room full of people: single women, couples with children, retired people, working people, former refugees, as well as people born in the United States. Most of them had read the same newspaper article I had, and they felt inexplicably drawn to finding out more.

We learned a lot that night: there are *thirteen million* refugees in the world today, most of them mothers and their children; there are another twenty-two million people internally displaced within the borders of their own countries due to civil war or other conflicts. Hundreds of thousands of children have been orphaned or separated from their parents and are at higher risk for abuse and exploitation. Many of the kids will live all of their childhood years in refugee camps.

After the meeting, Paul and I were a bit surprised when we each wanted to take the next step. We signed up to go through the foster parent certification process. During the following months, we met with refugees and heard unbelievable stories of courage and determination. I recognized how ignorant I was of the world and of the many refugees who were living in our own city. I was humbled by the unsung heroes I met, both the refugees, as well as the people who provide so many services to them.

One night after our monthly meeting, the director asked
us if we would be interested in becoming foster parents to a
seventeen-year-old girl from Iran. She was of the Bahá'í faith and
was granted refugee status because, in Iran, Bahá'í are often
persecuted or imprisoned, and the young people are not allowed
to go to college. She had been living on her own as a refugee in
Turkey since she was fifteen, and she needed a family when she
came to the United States.

We immediately said yes. We felt, from that very moment,
that she was part of our family. A month later, we went to the
airport to welcome Shima, our new daughter. Little did we know
how quickly we'd all fall in love with her. She has brought so
much joy and laughter into our home. Although she faces many
challenges ahead, we are committed to helping her through them.

Through this experience, the circle of our family has grown
larger. Our hearts and minds have expanded, not only in loving
Shima but also in learning first-hand about cultures and countries
very far away from our own. We meet each month with other
families and their refugee teens, and it is hard to put into words
how much this has changed us. We have grown to know and
care for these young people who have witnessed unspeakable

horrors in Sudan or Somalia, in Afghanistan or Sierra Leone. We are in awe of the fact that in the face of so much suffering, there is so much love.

Day by day we are discovering that, at the deepest level, all children are our own. As Mother Teresa invited us, let's draw the circle of our family large enough to hold them all. In ways big and small, let's make sure that all the children are cared for and loved. What could be more important than this?

Are All the Children In?

Pray or meditate on the phrase, "Are all the children in?" (Listen carefully; you might hear Momma Eternal whispering it in your heart.)

- With your children, look at a globe or a map at bedtime. Imagine drawing a circle of your family that includes all the animals and children and plants.
- Each night, you might choose a country and send special prayers to the children there.
- You might also decide together on some things you can do as a family for other children, whether in your own community or in another part of the world.

The Mother Is Standing

The practice of the presence of the Mother demands
and gives everything.
—Andrew Harvey, *Son of Man*

I was a goody-two-shoes for much of my life. I rarely broke
a rule, even a grammatical one. Although I've grown more comfortable with breaking rules as I've aged, the fact that I was about
to be arrested was still a stretch for me.

It was a beautiful Good Friday morning. Paul and I carpooled
with other members of our church community to a sunrise service,
held at the gates of Lawrence Livermore National Laboratory. We
had come to join with hundreds of other people—women and

men, nuns and priests, children, the healthy and the sick—to pray in quiet witness for peace as we walked the Stations of the Cross at the nuclear weapons facility.

We parked and walked toward the crowd gathering at the corner. Truck drivers driving by honked their support. I waved to men in black SUVs across the street, who sat sipping coffee and keeping an eye on things. Several unmarked helicopters buzzed overhead.

"I've *got* to go to the bathroom," I told Paul. I slogged through the mud to the blue port-a-potty that had been set up for our group's use. That was the first of five trips I would take to the bathroom.

Originally, I hadn't planned to participate in the civil disobedience. But earlier in the week, I woke up and heard myself say, "It's time for you to cross the line."

Those of us who were going to kneel in the road to the entrance of the lab wore cloth stoles around our necks. Other people wrote their names on our stoles, symbolizing that we were taking them all along with us. Paul wrote his name and our children's names on my stole, and the people from our church wrote theirs as well.

Our group moved together to the first Station and began to sing a familiar song. It was the *Stabat Mater,* which is Latin for "The Mother Was Standing." At each Station we sang it:

At the cross her station keeping,
Stood the mournful Mother weeping,
Close to Jesus to the last.

When I was a little girl, I attended Catholic elementary school, and each Friday during Lent, we processed over to the church to make the Stations of the Cross. At each station, we sang this song with its haunting melody; even then, it made me cry. A mother is staying with her son—her only child—as he is dying. Her heart is broken; she is unable to prevent his death, but she stays. She remains faithful in her great love for him.

She stayed. That's the thing. She stayed. The men ran away, fearing arrest, but the women stayed and the mother stayed. She stood with her son in silent and grieving witness. When she was pregnant with him, she was the mother who sang the Magnificat—that song of praise to the Holy One who sides with the poor and with those who suffer injustice. She had raised her son singing that prayer.

I didn't know it when I was a little girl, but this mother was becoming part of me; she was inviting me into her vision. She modeled how a mother stands, stays, bears witness, prays, and will not be moved.

That morning at the lab as we walked the fourteen Stations, we prayed and sang over and over, *Stabat Mater.* The Mother Was Standing. Finally, we arrived at the gate. There were so many men wearing suits; some worked at the lab, others at Homeland Security. There were even more riot police, dressed in full gear— helmets, reflective visors, bully sticks, mace. My stomach did a somersault. I said a quick prayer.

A line of fifteen riot police marched across the road by the gate, their boots pounding in unison. Ten members of our group filed quietly in front of them and then knelt in the road. From the sidelines, I looked at the police officers and was surprised to see how young they were. Most were not much older than my sons. They did not speak or look at anyone, although Paul, ever the comedian, got one to crack a smile at a joke.

Some members of our group weren't able to kneel because their knees were too arthritic. Several women had MS; they hobbled to their place on the road using their canes. One by one, each person was read the official demand to leave or be arrested.

One by one they refused. They were helped to their feet by an officer and escorted through the gates to be handcuffed and processed.

We began to sing a Taizé song, *Ubi Caritas*: "Where charity and love prevail, there is God." Over and over, we sang, and the music helped me to drop into my heart. I realized I wasn't afraid anymore. Crossing the line may not change what happens at the lab, but it had changed me. I knew that this was exactly where I needed to be: praying on this Good Friday with this little hobbled group of people, witnessing to the fact that we see, that we care, that we protest the normal way of doing things, that we believe in resurrection. I looked at the faces of the police and the lab officials and realized that it was likely that they, too, all wanted peace. I prayed for all of us.

As the first line emptied, I joined the second group and knelt in the road. After a few moments, an officer came to arrest me. A reporter from a local news station was there, and she put a microphone up to me as I was being led away. "Why are you doing this?" she asked. "For my children," I heard myself say.

The police took us to the side of the road, asked us to remove everything except our basic clothing, and then handcuffed us. Large white vans were waiting to take us to holding pens on the other side of the facility. As I got into one, I saw a friend of mine already in the back seat. He introduced me to others in the van, and we discovered that many of our paths had crossed before. We were taken to the outdoor pens, and ten or so people were locked up in each. The guards kindly brought folding chairs for the women with MS to sit on while they waited for processing.

Eventually, I was escorted into a large warehouse to be fingerprinted and photographed. There were tables set up, like at a college registration, and women sitting at different stations to take down our information. They issued me a citation and said that I would hear within several weeks whether the district attorney would prosecute. Then they took me to another, larger holding pen, where I met one of my professors from my seminary training twenty-five years ago. After a while, we were taken to another van, driven outside the gates, and released. I met Paul and our friends, and we left to go to our church's Good Friday service.

Our protest on that Good Friday morning did not change the world, at least as far as we can see. Nevertheless, it changed me, and it changed our community. A reporter once asked

A. J. Muste—a social activist who, during the Vietnam War, stood outside the White House night after night—"Mr. Muste, do you really think you are going to change the policies of this country by standing out here alone at night with a candle?"

"Oh," Muste replied. "I don't do this to change the country. I do this so the country won't change me."

When I am willing to cross the line of how much I think I can love, I am changed. When I am more in touch with what I love than with what I fear, I take a stand. My prayer is that more and more of us, on behalf of all children, will use the energy of a mother to touch the seeds of courage and love within us for the sake of the world.

The Mother Is Standing. And "the Mother" is a multitude when we stand together.

The Presence-of-the-Mother Practice

Go out at night and look at the stars. If you live in a city and it's hard to see the stars, light a candle for this prayer.

- Imagine that your children have children, and calculate what year it will be when your grandchildren will be eighty years old.
- Imagine that the world is at peace at that time.
- Listen to what your grandchildren might say to you now.
- Get a sense of your place as a mother in this moment between your ancestors and the future ones.
- Send a prayer across time.
- Ask for the grace of mothering, for the wisdom and courage and strength to nurture life and work toward a world of peace.

What Do Trees Have to Do with Peace?

The following is one mother's story. Her name is Wangari Maathai, and her story has been an inspiration to millions around the world. Although we may think, *We live far away from Africa; what does this have to do with my family?* Wangari shows us that we are one community, one earth, and we will be well only if we care for each other and for the earth.

Thirty years ago, in the country of Kenya, 90 percent of the forest had been chopped down. Without trees to hold the topsoil in place, the land became like a desert. When the women and girls went in search of firewood in order to prepare the meals, they had to spend hours and hours looking for what few branches remained.

A woman named Wangari watched all this happening. She decided that there must be a way to take better care of the land and take better care of the women and girls. So she planted a tree. And then she planted another. She wanted to plant thousands of trees, but she realized that it would take a very long time if she were the only one doing it. So she taught the women who were looking for firewood to plant trees, and they were paid a small amount for each sapling they grew.

Soon she organized women all over the country to plant trees, and a movement took hold. It was called the Green Belt Movement, and with each passing year, more and more trees covered the land.

But something else was happening as the women planted those trees. Something else besides those trees was taking root.

The women began to have confidence in themselves. They began to see that they could make a difference. They began to see that they were capable of many things and that they were equal to the men. They began to recognize that they were deserving of being treated with respect and dignity.

Changes like these were threatening to some. The president of the country didn't like any of this. So police were sent to intimidate and beat Wangari for planting trees and for planting ideas of equality and democracy in people's heads, especially women's. She was accused of subversion and arrested many times.

One time, while Wangari was trying to plant trees, land developers hired guards who clubbed her, and she was hospitalized with head injuries. But she survived, and it only made her realize that she was on the right path.

For almost thirty years, she was threatened physically, and she was often made fun of in the press. But she didn't flinch. She only had to look in the eyes of her three children and in the eyes of the thousands of women and girls who were blossoming right along with the trees, and she found the strength to continue.

And that is how it came to be that thirty million trees have been planted in Africa, one tree at a time. The landscapes—both the external one of the land and the internal one of the people—have been transformed.

In 2002, the people of Kenya held a democratic election, and the president and ruling party who opposed Wangari and her Green Belt Movement were voted out of office. Wangari became Kenya's assistant minister for the environment.

After her appointment to the government, she told the U.N. Environmental Programme:

> Our recent experience in Kenya gives hope to all who have been struggling for a better future. It shows it is possible to bring about positive change, and still do it peacefully. All it takes is courage and perseverance, and a belief that positive change is possible. That is why the slogan for our campaign was "Yote Yaawezekana!" or "It is Possible!"

Wangari is now in her late sixties. In 2004, she became the first African woman to be awarded the Nobel Peace Prize. After she was notified, she gave a speech titled, "What Do Trees Have to Do with Peace?" She pointed out how most wars are fought over limited natural resources, such as oil, land, coltan, or diamonds. She called for an end to corporate greed and for leaders to build more just societies. She added:

> On behalf of all African women, I want to express my profound appreciation for this honour, which will serve to encourage women in Kenya, in Africa, and around the world to raise their voices and not to be deterred . . . we plant trees, we plant the seeds of peace and seeds of hope. We also secure the future for our children.

When she received the Nobel Peace Prize in Oslo, she invited all of us to get involved:

> Today we are faced with a challenge that calls for a shift in our thinking, so that humanity stops threatening its life-support system. . . . We are called to assist the Earth to heal her wounds and in the process heal our own—indeed, to embrace the whole creation in all its diversity, beauty and wonder. This will happen if we see the need to revive our sense of belonging to a larger family of life.

Can we accept Wangari's invitation? How might we do the equivalent of planting one tree?

Planting Trees

In an interview, Wangari said,

> I don't really know why I care so much. I just have something inside me
> that tells me that there is a problem and I have got to do something about it. I
> think that is what I would call the God in me. It must be this voice that is
> telling me to do something, and I am sure it is the same voice that is speaking
> to everybody on this planet.

Take some time to meditate.

What might that voice be speaking to you?

As you look around your neighborhood or city or country, what is needed?

Where are women and children suffering?

Where are people feeling disempowered?

Where does the earth need your help?

What is your equivalent of planting one tree?

A Final Word

When I was a little girl, I sometimes had trouble sleeping. One night my mother suggested that I pray as a way of quieting my mind and body. It worked so well that I fell asleep right in the middle of my prayers. The next morning, I went to her, distressed. Because I hadn't finished them, I wasn't sure my prayers had counted.

"Oh, honey, it's OK," she said. "Let me tell you about the Angels' Promise. All you have to do is begin your prayers. Then if for some reason you can't complete them, the angels will finish them for you."

I remember the Angels' Promise now as I come to the end of this book. The words on these pages are the continuation of a prayer that began the moment I first found out I was pregnant, over two and a half decades ago.

As my children have grown and have begun to leave home, I've come to believe that the Angels' Promise holds true for mothers as well. Our part is to begin the work with our children. In the end, that's all we can do. Then we must let go, say a prayer, and trust the universe—and all the angels—to hold them.

Mothering is a vocation that stretches us and that helps us find that which is most wise and loving and generous within us. Day by day, we deepen our practice of Momfulness by being more present, attentive, compassionate, embodied, in touch with the sacred, and committed to community. As we open to the immense and maternal love at the heart of the universe, we discover that all of life becomes a meditation that transforms us, our families, and our world.

Let us keep reminding each other to breathe, to smile, to treat ourselves and one another with kindness. Let us hold each other when we need support, and let us challenge and remind each other of what is truly important. Let us take care of ourselves so that we don't hand down our unfinished business to the next generation. Let us laugh together, and never lose our joy.

And let us take care of the children—our children, all the children. Let us mobilize our fierce and passionate mother energy on behalf of all beings on this little blue-green planet we call Mother Earth.

In closing, I offer this blessing:

May we be fully present, here and now, aware of the gift of
    each moment.
May we pay attention with kindness to what is happening
    within us and within our children.
May our hearts open wide with compassion for ourselves,
    our children, and our world.
May we live fully in our bodies as we bless our families each day.
May we open to the great love and grace that holds us all.
May we care for each other and for the earth as we draw wide
    the circle of our family.
May we all find peace.
May we all be well.

Suggested Reading

Baldwin, Christina. *Life's Companion.* New York: Bantam Books, 1991.

Barrows, Anita, and Macy, Joanna. *Rilke's Book of Hours.* New York: Riverhead Books, 1996.

Bolen, Jean Shinoda. *Urgent Message from Mother.* York Beach, Maine: Conari Press, 2005.

Borba, Michele. *12 Simple Secrets Real Moms Know.* San Francisco: Jossey-Bass, 2006.

Brach, Tara. *Radical Acceptance.* New York: Bantam Books, 2003.

Bria, Gina. *The Art of Family.* New York: Dell, 1998.

Chödrön, Pema. *The Places That Scare You.* Boston: Shambhala, 2001.

Cox, Meg. *The Book of New Family Traditions.* Philadelphia: Running Press Book Publishers, 2003.

Dillard, Annie. *Pilgrim at Tinker Creek.* New York: Harper's Magazine Press, 1974.

Doe, Mimi. *10 Principles for Spiritual Parenting.* New York: HarperPerennial, 1998.

Duerk, Judith. *Circle of Stones.* Philadelphia: Innisfree Press, 1999.

Ferrucci, Piero. *What Our Children Teach Us.* New York: Warner Books, 2001.

Ford-Grabowsky, Mary. *WomanPrayers.* San Francisco: HarperSanFrancisco, 2003.

Fox, John. *Poetic Medicine.* New York: Jeremy P. Tarcher/Putnam, 1997. (www.poeticmedicine.org)

Gore, Ariel. *The Mother Trip.* Seattle: Seal Press, 2000.

Hanh, Thich Nhat. *Peace Is Every Step.* New York: Bantam Books, 1991.

Hirshfield, Jane. *Women in Praise of the Sacred.* New York: HarperPerennial, 1995.

Huber, Cheri, and Guyol, Melinda. *Time-Out for Parents.* Murphys, Calif.: Keep It Simple Press, 2004.

Jensen, Derrick. *Listening to the Land.* San Francisco: Sierra Club Books, 1995.

Kabat-Zinn, Myla, and Kabat-Zinn, Jon. *Everyday Blessings.* New York: Hyperion, 1997.

Kenison, Katrina. *Mitten Strings for God.* New York: Warner Books, 2000.

Kidd, Sue Monk. *The Dance of the Dissident Daughter.* San Francisco: HarperSanFrancisco, 1996.

Kidd, Sue Monk. *The Secret Life of Bees.* New York: Penguin, 2003.

Kingston, Karen. *Clear Your Clutter with Feng Shui.* New York: Broadway Books, 1999.

Kornfield, Jack. *A Path with Heart.* New York: Bantam Books, 1993.

Ladinsky, Daniel. *Love Poems from God.* New York: Penguin Compass, 2002.

Lamott, Anne. *Operating Instructions.* New York: Pantheon Books, 1993.

Lamott, Anne. *Traveling Mercies.* New York: Pantheon Books, 1999.

Lerner, Harriet. *The Mother Dance.* New York: HarperPerennial, 1999.

Lewis, Thomas, Amini, Fari, and Lannon, Richard. *A General Theory of Love.* New York: Random House, 2000.

Lindbergh, Anne Morrow. *Gift from the Sea.* New York: Pantheon, 1975.

Louv, Richard. *Last Child in the Woods.* Chapel Hill, N.C.: Algonquin Books of Chapel Hill, 2005.

Muller, Wayne. *Sabbath.* New York: Bantam Books, 2000.

Oliver, Mary. *Dream Work.* Boston: Atlantic Monthly Press, 1986.

Palmer, Parker. *Let Your Life Speak.* San Francisco: Jossey-Bass, 2000.

Pipher, Mary. *The Shelter of Each Other.* New York: Putnam, 1996.

Pipher, Mary. *The Middle of Everywhere.* Orlando: Harcourt Brace, 2002.

Remen, Rachel Naomi. *Kitchen Table Wisdom.* New York: Riverhead Books, 1996.

Roy, Denise. *My Monastery Is a Minivan.* Chicago: Loyola Press, 2001.

Salzberg, Sharon. *Lovingkindness.* Boston: Shambhala, 1995.

Saso, Patt, and Saso, Steve. *Parenting Your Teens with T.L.C.* Notre Dame, Ind.: Sorin Books, 2005.

Siegel, Daniel, and Hartzell, Mary. *Parenting from the Inside Out.* New York: J.P. Tarcher/Putnam, 2003.

Tolle, Eckhart. *The Power of Now.* Novato, Calif.: New World Library, 2001.

Ueland, Brenda. *If You Want to Write.* New York: Putnam, 1938.

Wheatley, Margaret. *Finding Our Way.* San Francisco: Berrett-Koehler, 2005.

Whyte, David. *The House of Belonging.* Langley, Wash.: Many Rivers Press, 1997.

Williams, Terry Tempest. *Refuge.* New York: Vintage Books, 1992.

Williams, Terry Tempest. *The Open Space of Democracy.* Great Barrington, Mass.: Orion Society, 2004.

Check Denise Roy's Web site for additional resources, including CDs, tapes, and links to other Web sites, at www.DeniseRoy.com.

Acknowledgments

have been blessed by the support of many people. I am so grateful for good friends: Debbie Marsella, Patt and Steve Saso, Sr. Barbara Williams, Christine Evans, Nick Ross, Ed Morgan, Seán ÓLaoire, and all the members of my faith community who are too numerous to name. I thank you for your love and wisdom and generosity of spirit.

My mother, Jeanne Cryan, loves her children and grand-children so much, and I am thankful for all she has taught me. My sisters, Nancy Freschi and Teresa Souvignier, are both mothers extraordinaire, and I am blessed to have them in my life. My sister-in-law, Suzanne Roy, is a talented editor and creative coach, and she generously shared her gifts with me in the writing of this book.

My appreciation goes to those friends who contributed ideas and insights to this book. Amy Saltzman, M.D., offered encouragement, as well as mindful parenting practices, including "Late-for-School Practice." Debby Maguire shared so many stories and her own "Ponytail Practice," and Carolyn Foster, who long ago helped shape my writing vision, generously shared the "Saved by Wonder" story. I am grateful, too, to the many mothers who have attended my talks and seminars and have shared their hopes and their challenges. They are a great inspiration.

Thanks to all on the publishing end who helped make this book a reality: to my literary agent, Tom Grady, who believed in the book when all I had was an idea and a title; to my fabulous editor, Julianna Gustafson, whose energy, enthusiasm, and thoughtful guidance were invaluable, and to all the folks at Jossey-Bass, including Catherine Craddock, Andrea Flint, Joanne Clapp Fullagar, Sandy Siegle, and the many other members of the team.

My deep gratitude goes to Catholic Charities of San Jose and Adopt International, who have partnered to establish the Unaccompanied Refugee Minor program; they have brought

Shima into our family, and they have made possible a hopeful future for so many others. Special thanks to Sr. Marilyn Lacey, Coleen Higa Gulbraa, Terry Watters, Theresa Samuel-Boko, Sr. Kathleen Connoll, and Gilah Abelson.

I am forever grateful for my children. Ben, David, Matt, Julianna, and Shima are great gifts to me and to this world. Anything I've learned about Momfulness, I've learned from them. Finally, my eternal thanks go to my husband, Paul, for his love and laughter and support and encouragement. I am incredibly blessed to have him as my life partner. *Je t'aime.*

The Author

Denise Roy is the author of the award-winning *My Monastery Is a Minivan* and is in private practice as a licensed marriage and family therapist. She holds a Master of Arts degree in counseling psychology, as well as a Master of Divinity degree.

Denise speaks nationally on parenting, spirituality, peacemaking, and women's issues. She and her husband have three sons and two daughters; they live in Northern California. To contact Denise about her talks, workshops, retreats, or consulting, visit her Web site at www.DeniseRoy.com.

Other Books of Interest

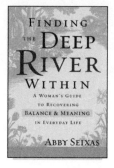

Finding the Deep River Within

A Woman's Guide to Recovering Balance & Meaning in Everyday Life

Abby Seixas

Cloth
ISBN 10: 0-7879-8097-8
ISBN 13: 978-0-7879-8097-9

"*Finding the Deep River Within* holds the key to lasting health and sustainable joy."
    —CHRISTIANE NORTHRUP, M.D., author, *Mother-Daughter Wisdom,*
        The Wisdom of Menopause, and *Women's Bodies, Women's Wisdom*

"In *Finding the Deep River Within,* Abby Seixas gives us a wisdom-filled recipe for living a soulful life. This is a book for Everywoman, at least every woman living in our nonstop, do-it-all culture. There is not a woman I know who wouldn't benefit from this valuable book."
    —JACK CANFIELD, cocreator of the *Chicken Soup for the Soul* series; coauthor,
        The Success Principles: How to Get from Where You Are to Where You Want to Be

This gentle and practical guide will help women escape their to-do lists so that they can reconnect with the source of life and spirit—the deep river of their inner lives. The book offers a proven, step-by-step program that shows how to slow down and recover a sense of depth, balance, and meaning, providing women with practical ways to simplify their overscheduled lives and achieve greater satisfaction, and find the spirit, calmness, and wisdom that flows within them.

Abby Seixas has been a psychotherapist in private practice for over twenty-five years, working as a consultant and clinical psychotherapy supervisor at training centers in the United States and abroad, including England, the Netherlands, and Russia. For the last twelve years, her work has focused on helping women learn and practice the art of slowing down through public talks, retreats, workshops, individual coaching, and her popular Touching the Deep River groups. She is the mother of two grown children and lives with her husband near Boston, Massachusetts.

Other Books of Interest

12 Simple Secrets Real Moms Know
Getting Back to Basics and Raising Happy Kids
Michele Borba

Paper
ISBN 10: 0-7879-8096-X
ISBN 13: 978-0-7879-8096-2

"Balance and going with the flow goes far beyond just figure skating for me. It's the core of my athletic career and the core of my personal life. Everyone talks about living a healthy lifestyle, but that also applies to parenting style. Dr. Borba's book is the journey of healthy parenting— heart-warming and at times heart-wrenching. Every reader of this book is sure to have an "ah-ha!" moment and rediscover the simple joys of parenting."

—PEGGY FLEMING JENKINS, 1968 Olympic champion/ABC sports commentator

"A revolutionary, wonderful, and welcome answer to a mother's prayers. Michele Borba has shown us all how to be loving moms who raise great kids, without losing our peace of mind, our lives as adults, or our true selves."

—PHYLLIS GEORGE, former Miss America, pioneer female sportscaster, former first lady of Kentucky, and mother

Best-selling parenting guru Michele Borba, the mother of three, has surveyed 5,000 mothers for their experience and wisdom in raising happier, more confident kids by returning to a more natural, authentic kind of mothering. She shares 12 top secrets of successful moms culled from her research and shows how to apply them to your family.

Michele Borba, Ed.D., recipient of the National Educator Award, is the author of *Nobody Likes Me, Everybody Hates Me; Don't Give Me That Attitude!; No More Misbehavin'; Parents Do Make a Difference;* and *Building Moral Intelligence,* all from Jossey-Bass. She appears regularly on talk shows, including the Today show, the View, and the Early Show. Visit her on the Web at www.micheleborba.com.